Better Homes and Gardens®

America's Best
Cross-Stitch

BETTER HOMES AND GARDENS® BOOKS

Editor: Gerald M. Knox
Art Director: Ernest Shelton
Managing Editor: David A. Kirchner
Editorial Project Managers: James D. Blume,
    Marsha Jahns, Rosanne Weber Mattson,
    Mary Helen Schiltz

Crafts Editor: Joan Cravens
Senior Crafts Editors: Beverly Rivers, Sara Jane Treinen
Associate Crafts Editor: Liz Porter

Associate Art Directors: Neoma Thomas,
    Linda Ford Vermie, Randall Yontz
Assistant Art Directors: Lynda Haupert,
    Harijs Priekulis, Tom Wegner
Graphic Designers: Mike Burns, Brian Wignall
Art Production: Director, John Berg;
    Associate, Joe Heuer;
    Office Manager: Michaela Lester

President, Book Group: Fred Stines
Vice President, General Manager: Jeramy Lanigan
Vice President, Retail Marketing: Jamie L. Martin
Vice President, Administrative Services: Rick Rundall

BETTER HOMES AND GARDENS® MAGAZINE
President, Magazine Group: James A. Autry
Vice President, Editorial Director: Doris Eby
Executive Director, Editorial Services: Duane L. Gregg

MEREDITH CORPORATE OFFICERS
Chairman of the Board: E.T. Meredith III
President: Robert A. Burnett
Executive Vice President: Jack D. Rehm

America's Best Cross-Stitch
Contributing Editor: Gary Boling
Editorial Project Manager: Marsha Jahns
Graphic Designer: Brian Wignall
Electronic Text Processor: Cindy Cox

Cover project: See page 16.

ook at all of the projects in America's Best Cross-Stitch *and you'll see why cross-stitch is the craft that everyone wants to do. The techniques are easy to master, the materials are inexpensive and easy to find, and the possibilities are limitless. Whether you're a beginner or an old hand at cross-stitching, you'll find beautiful designs for every occasion and setting, from traditional samplers to lively contemporary motifs. Create cross-stitch projects to decorate every room in your house, to surprise someone with a lovely gift you've made yourself, to celebrate special occasions and holidays in grand style, and—above all— to satisfy your own creative spirit.*

CONTENTS

Simple Stitches, Spectacular Treasures

Fabulous Florals

An armload of freshly picked summer flowers has inspired many artists, and those sweet bouquets haven't gone unnoticed by cross-stitchers.

Floral designs depicted in cross-stitch embroidery are the hands-down favorite for embellishing linens and home accessories. It's easy to see why—graceful stems, leaves, and petals are natural shapes to transpose into embroidery. The black-eyed susan and bluebell motifs on this cross-stitched afghan are just two of the flowers featured in the Prairie Blooms chapter, which begins on page 14.

Instructions for this afghan begin on page 31.

Simple Stitches, Spectacular Treasures

Samplers Old and New

Although today's cross-stitchers create samplers of all sorts, their work developed from a centuries-old practice of recording and perfecting stitches and designs on scraps of fabric. Over the years, samplers have evolved from utilitarian practice pieces into decorative pictures and commemorative designs celebrating important occasions and special events. But even the most contemporary samplers continue to be artful combinations of alphabets, borders, and individual motifs. Whether you prefer to create traditional samplers inspired by treasured antiques, or more free-spirited designs, you'll find a wealth of patterns in this book.

Instructions for the Woodland Blossoms Sampler shown here begin on page 126.

Spirited Keepsakes

Making and exchanging handmade keepsakes are part of the appeal of perfecting a craft, and cross-stitch is brimming with rewarding possibilities. The adaptability of cross-stitch enables you to create small stitcheries that have all the qualities and impact of larger, more complicated designs.

This heart ornament and pair of sachets illustrate the artistic qualities of cross-stitch. The towel, embroidered along one edge, shows how cross-stitch satisfies an eye for detail. In contrast, the teddy bear and the folk-art rabbit demonstrate lively forms of cross-stitch.

Instructions for the heart and rabbit begin on page 176. To make a flower-trimmed towel, see the instructions on page 129. Three more animal designs accompany the bear, page 93. A chapter of home accessories, including the ornament, begins on page 62.

Simple Stitches, Spectacular Treasures

Personal Style

Many cross-stitch designers feel that creating a successful design is as easy as A-B-C. That's because the alphabet turns up more often in cross-stitch embroidery than in any other craft.

Stitching a letter or two onto anything is easy with cross-stitch. And you'll find more than a dozen alphabets in this book to monogram any item with the right size and style of letter.

The pillow sham and candle screen shown here are among several accessories that incorporate one of the alphabets from this book. You can create your own patterns by combining a letter with a border design, or by using letters alone.

Graph paper and colored pencils or markers are all you need to design your own patterns. Consult our chapter of cross-stitch tips and techniques, pages 180–187, to get started.

Prairie Blooms

Nothing can compare to the profusion of blooms found on a sun-drenched prairie. This chapter contains designs based on flowers common to our country's grasslands, from black-eyed susans to wild strawberries.

Here's a cheery spot for morning coffee! The sampler, *opposite*, features flower motifs used for the projects shown here—tabletop accessories and a pillow brimming with strawberries.

Patterns and instructions for these and more projects begin on page 24.

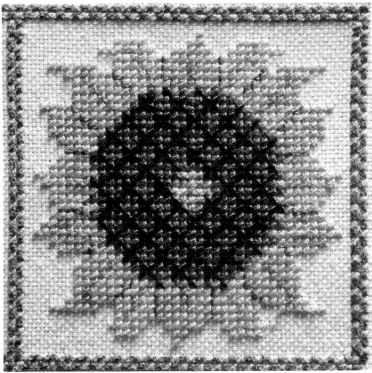

his magnificent sampler, *opposite,* is a tour de force in cross-stitch. Its vivid colors and lively branching foliage are balanced by a symmetrical plan and mirror-image motifs.

The sampler is framed by borders stitched in a yellow and bronze-color checkerboard pattern. The outer motifs are black-eyed susans and bluebells gathered into an L-shape motif in each corner and a straight design along the sides.

Inside this border four sunflowers define the spaces for the inner group of flowers. Clusters of pink prairie roses fall into the adjacent rectangular spaces at the top and bottom, and on both sides. In the center of the sampler three stacked rectangles are filled with, from top to bottom, a coneflower, three thistles, and a pair of strawberry vines.

The apron hanging on the chair, *left,* illustrates how just one or two of the sampler's motifs can be incorporated in other accessories. Simply stitch a black-eyed susan and bluebell motif onto a piece of even-weave fabric. Then use a commercial pattern from a fabric store to complete the project.

his trio of projects based on the prairie rose motif is equally striking stitched on black or on white fabrics.

A plaid blanket is beautifully enhanced by cross-stitched edging, *left.* Stitching the single and double rose motifs to closely match the width of a blanket requires a little planning before you begin stitching, but the effect is well worth the additional preparation time.

When a single rose motif is centered and stitched above the double rose motif, the resulting design is ideal for a tea cozy. The cozy, *opposite*—a gracious and practical table accessory—is stitched on black hardanger.

A single prairie rose is just right for the napkin caddy, *opposite.* It's designed to add a bit of color to a casual place setting, and can substitute for a decorated place mat.

ovely enough to be used alone, the black-eyed susan and bluebell motifs are just right as a stitched border on a variety of projects.

The square tablecloth, *opposite,* is luncheon-cloth size. This version is stitched on white hardanger, but the motifs would be just as striking stitched on a rich green or beautiful deep blue fabric. Because the corner motifs do not extend an equal distance along two adjacent edges, each corner motif is rotated a quarter-turn so that the finished tablecloth is square. For larger cloths, hardanger is available in widths of more than 60 inches; see if a stitchery supply store can custom-order a piece sufficiently large for rectangular or oval tables.

A handmade panel of afghan crochet forms the background for the afghan, *above.* Six black-eyed susan and bluebell motifs provide the cross-stitch decoration—one in each corner and one on each long side.

Instead of crocheting the background panel, purchase large even-weave fabric throws designed to be decorated with cross-stitch. Then, using graph paper and markers, chart an adaptation of this idea to stitch along the throw's edges.

Prairie Blooms

mall designs are most effective when used in multiples. Here are two ways to repeat a simple pattern with spectacular results.

Trim a mirror, *right,* with 14 repeats of the thistle motif from the sampler on page 16. For variations, just change the number of motifs and their placement to make a rectangle to fit in any size of mirror frame.

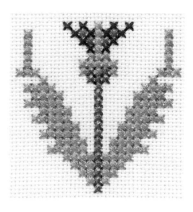

Or, work nine repeats of the wild strawberry design on the front of a ruffled pillow, *opposite.* As a whimsical touch, reverse the center strawberry.

Any of the central motifs from the sampler—and many of the other samplers in this book—are appropriate for pillow covers. See pages 184–185 for more information on creating your own designs from our basic patterns.

Prairie Blooms

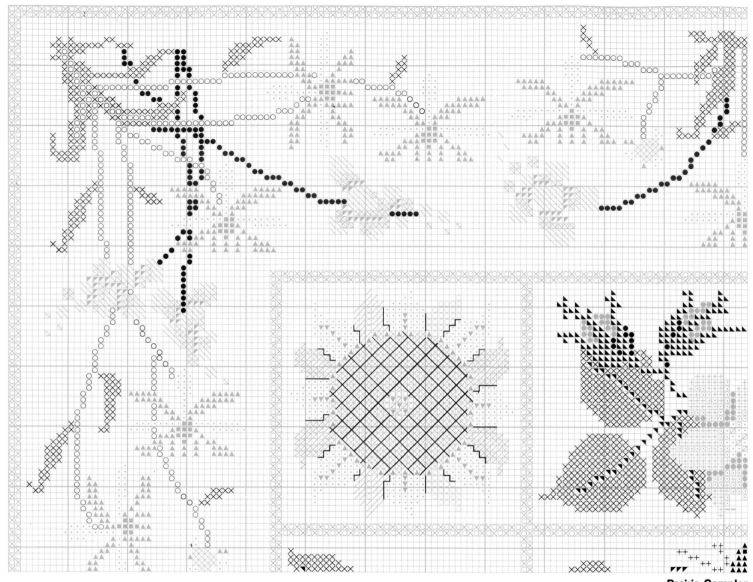

Prairie Sampler

COLOR KEY

- ⊠ Light Avocado Leaf Green (831)
- ⬚ Light Old Gold (676)
- ⊠ Medium Parrot Green (906)
- ◮ Light Tangerine (742)
- ◉ Deep Parrot Green (904)
- ● Seafoam Green (562)
- ◸ Pale Delft Blue (800)
- ◣ Dark Forest Green (987)

- ⊡ Medium Watermelon (3706)
- ■ Black (310)
- ⬚ Dark Lemon Yellow (444)
- ◪ Medium Yellow (743)
- ◩ Royal Blue (797)
- ◫ Medium Delft Blue (799)
- ⬣ Watermelon (3705)
- ⊞ Light Watermelon (3708)

- ⊡ White
- ◪ Periwinkle Blue (333)
- ◨ Dark Shell Gray (451)
- ◩ Deep Violet (550)
- ⊞ Dark Violet (552)
- ◤ Light Violet (554)
- ◣ Medium Seafoam Green (563)
- ◪ Deep Beige-Gray (640)

- ◿ Topaz (725)
- ▽ Light Olive Green (734)
- ▦ Dark Coffee Brown (801)
- ⬚ Garnet (816)
- ▲ Deep Coffee Brown (898)
- ◿ Medium Plum (917)
- ⊠ Forest Green (989)
- ◺ Aquamarine (992)

24

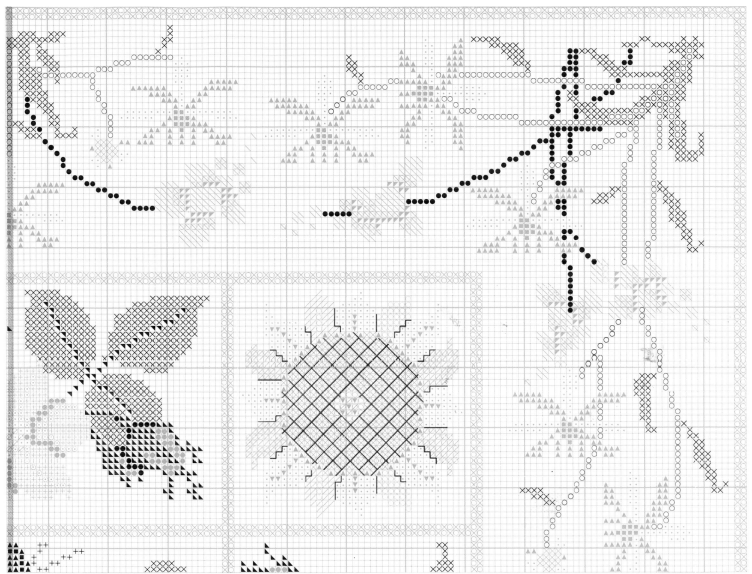

Prairie Sampler

Prairie Blooms

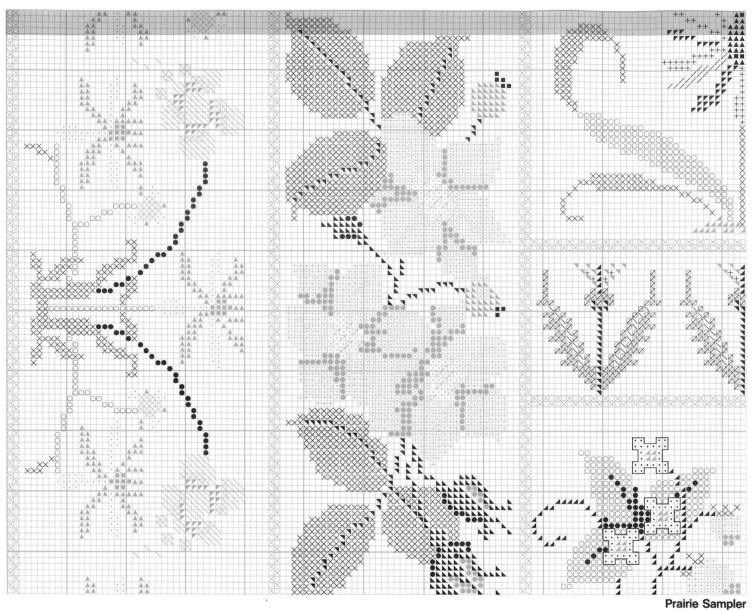

Prairie Sampler

COLOR KEY

⊠ Light Avocado Leaf Green (831)
▢ Light Old Gold (676)
⊠ Medium Parrot Green (906)
▲ Light Tangerine (742)
◎ Deep Parrot Green (904)
● Seafoam Green (562)
◩ Pale Delft Blue (800)
◣ Dark Forest Green (987)

⊡ Medium Watermelon (3706)
■ Black (310)
⊡ Dark Lemon Yellow (444)
▨ Medium Yellow (743)
◪ Royal Blue (797)
◩ Medium Delft Blue (799)
◉ Watermelon (3705)
⊞ Light Watermelon (3708)

· White
◪ Periwinkle Blue (333)
◨ Dark Shell Gray (451)
◳ Deep Violet (550)
⊞ Dark Violet (552)
◿ Light Violet (554)
◣ Medium Seafoam Green (563)
◪ Deep Beige-Gray (640)

▨ Topaz (725)
▽ Light Olive Green (734)
▦ Dark Coffee Brown (801)
◣ Garnet (816)
▲ Deep Coffee Brown (898)
▨ Medium Plum (917)
▨ Forest Green (989)
◳ Aquamarine (992)

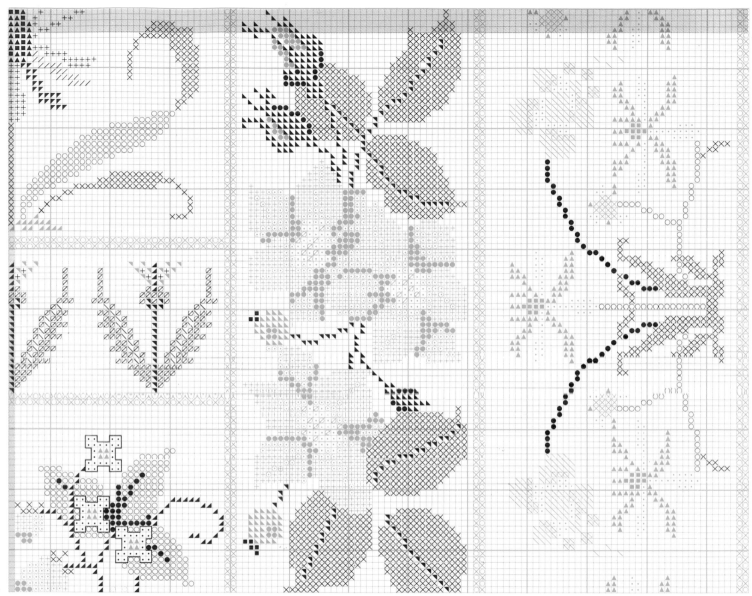

Prairie Sampler

Prairie Blooms

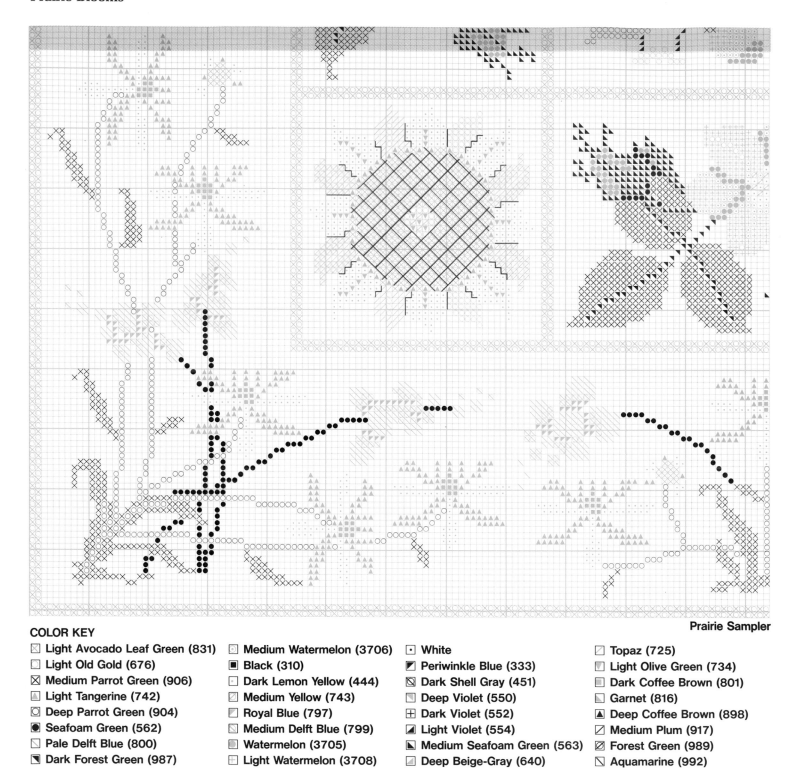

Prairie Sampler

COLOR KEY

⊠ Light Avocado Leaf Green (831)
▢ Light Old Gold (676)
⊠ Medium Parrot Green (906)
▲ Light Tangerine (742)
◎ Deep Parrot Green (904)
◉ Seafoam Green (562)
◺ Pale Delft Blue (800)
◣ Dark Forest Green (987)

◨ Medium Watermelon (3706)
◼ Black (310)
⊡ Dark Lemon Yellow (444)
◲ Medium Yellow (743)
◳ Royal Blue (797)
◲ Medium Delft Blue (799)
◼ Watermelon (3705)
⊞ Light Watermelon (3708)

⊡ White
◤ Periwinkle Blue (333)
◲ Dark Shell Gray (451)
◼ Deep Violet (550)
⊞ Dark Violet (552)
◿ Light Violet (554)
◣ Medium Seafoam Green (563)
◺ Deep Beige-Gray (640)

◹ Topaz (725)
◥ Light Olive Green (734)
◼ Dark Coffee Brown (801)
◺ Garnet (816)
▲ Deep Coffee Brown (898)
◿ Medium Plum (917)
⊠ Forest Green (989)
◺ Aquamarine (992)

28

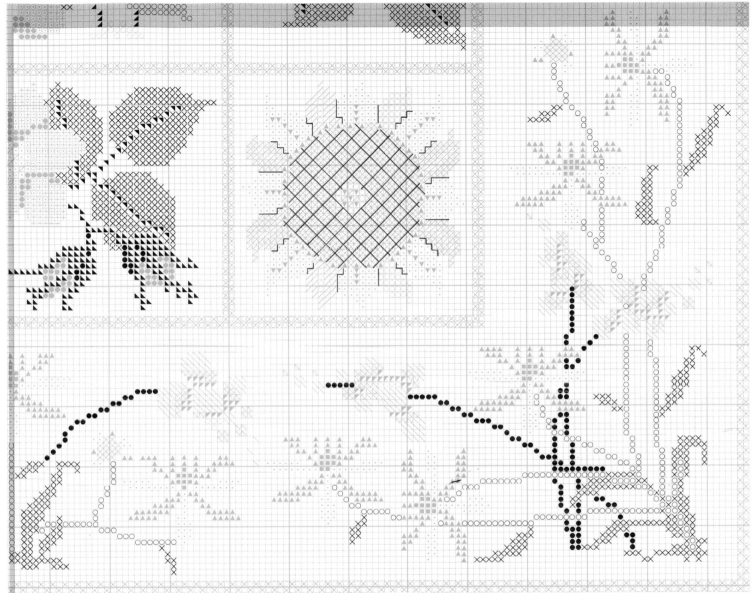

Prairie Sampler

Sampler

Shown on page 16.
Finished size of stitchery is 22½x25⅜ inches.
Design is 247 stitches wide and 279 stitches high.

MATERIALS
40x45-inch piece of white hardanger
DMC embroidery floss: 6 skeins of
  light avocado leaf green (831); 5
  skeins *each* of light old gold (676)
  and medium parrot green (906); 4
  skeins *each* of light tangerine (742)
  and deep parrot green (904); 3
  skeins *each* of seafoam green
  (562), pale delft blue (800), dark
  forest green (987), and medium
  watermelon (3706); 2 skeins *each*
  of black (310), dark lemon yellow
  (444), medium yellow (743), royal
  blue (797), medium delft blue (799),
  watermelon (3705), and light
  watermelon (3708); and 1 skein
  each of white, dark periwinkle
  blue (333), dark shell gray (451),
  deep violet (550), dark violet (552),
  light violet (554), medium seafoam
  green (563), deep beige-gray (640),
  topaz (725), light olive green (734),
  dark coffee brown (801), garnet
  (816), deep coffee brown (898),
  medium plum (917), forest green
  (989), and aquamarine (992)
Embroidery hoop
Tapestry needle

INSTRUCTIONS
  Before beginning, see the general information on pages 180–183 for special cross-stitch tips and techniques.
  Referring to the patterns, pages 24–
29, chart design onto graph paper using felt-tip markers. Tape several
sheets of graph paper together, if desired, or plan to stitch from smaller
sheets. See diagram, *above,* for positioning patterns from the six pages to
complete entire design.

Page 24	Page 25
Page 26	Page 27
Page 28	Page 29

  Use three plies of floss and work
the cross-stitches over two threads of
hardanger. Measure 8 inches down
from the top and 8 inches in from the
left side; begin stitching upper-left corner of border here.
  When working backstitches in center of sunflower use black (310). Use
light avocado leaf green (831) for outline between sunflower petals. Outline white strawberry blossoms with
backstitches worked in deep parrot
green (904).
  Steam-press the stitchery on the
wrong side.
  Frame the sampler as desired.

Tablecloth

Shown on page 20.
Finished size is 39½x39½ inches.

MATERIALS
42x42-inch piece of white hardanger
DMC embroidery floss: 4 skeins *each*
  of dark lemon yellow (444), light
  tangerine (742), and medium
  parrot green (906); 3 skeins *each*
  of pale delft blue (800) and deep

parrot green (904); 2 skeins *each*
  of seafoam green (562), royal blue
  (797), and medium delft blue (799);
  and 1 skein *each* of dark coffee
  brown (801) and light avocado leaf
  green (831)
Embroidery hoop, tapestry needle

INSTRUCTIONS
  Before beginning, see the general information on pages 180–183 for special cross-stitch tips and techniques.
  Referring to the pattern for the sampler, pages 24–29, chart the black-
eyed susan and bluebell motif that
appears in the upper-right corner of
the sampler on graph paper with felt-
tip markers. Then chart the adjacent
straight motif. This motif is also used
for the apron on page 20 (instructions
begin opposite); chart the motif either
from the sampler pattern, pages 24–29,
or from the apron pattern, *opposite.*
The corner motif is basically an L
shape and the straight motif from the
apron bib is basically a rectangle. Use
this as the master pattern for the
tablecloth.
  Use three plies of floss and work
the cross-stitches over two threads of
hardanger. Measure 2 inches down
from the top and 2 inches in from the
right. Begin stitching the corner motif
here. When corner motif is completed,
stitch the adjacent straight motifs directly to the left and directly beneath
the corner motif. At this point, baste
lines along the bottom of the straight
motifs to position remaining motifs.
  Then repeat straight motif once
more on top and right sides, leaving a
stitch between motifs. (*Note:* All three
straight motifs along a side, if stitched
correctly, will be repeat patterns.)
  To complete the upper-right corner,
turn the master pattern a quarter-turn
counterclockwise. Stitch the next
straight motif from the master pattern,
then the corner motif, and finally the
remaining straight motif to begin the
left side. For the lower-left corner,

turn the master pattern a quarter-turn *clockwise*. Stitch the next straight motif, then the corner motif, and finally the remaining straight motif to begin the bottom side. At this point, again baste lines along the bottom edge of the straight motifs. Stitch two more of the straight motifs—one adjacent to each of the straight motifs just stitched—again leaving one stitch between motifs.

To complete final corner, turn the master pattern *two* quarter-turns in either direction, and stitch the fourth corner and remaining two straight motifs.

Hem 1 inch beyond basting lines.

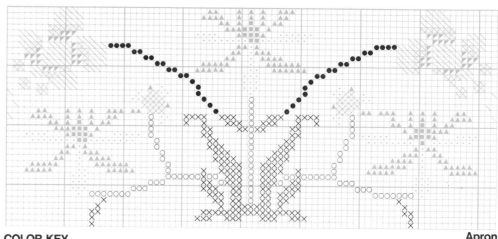

Apron

COLOR KEY

☐ Dark Lemon Yellow (444)	☐ Pale Delft Blue (800)
◉ Seafoam Green (562)	▨ Dark Coffee Brown (801)
▲ Light Tangerine (742)	⊠ Light Avocado Leaf Green (831)
▨ Royal Blue (797)	◎ Deep Parrot Green (904)
◹ Medium Delft Blue (799)	⊠ Medium Parrot Green (906)

Apron

Shown on page 20.

MATERIALS

Commercial apron pattern with bib (*Note:* Finished size of bib must be at least 8 inches wide)
DMC embroidery floss: 1 skein *each* of dark lemon yellow (444), seafoam green (562), light tangerine (742), royal blue (797), medium delft blue (799), pale delft blue (800), dark coffee brown (801), light avocado leaf green (831), deep parrot green (904), and medium parrot green (906)
White hardanger sufficiently large for bib piece, plus 2 inches all around
Fabric necessary for apron, according to pattern envelope instructions
Water-erasable marking pen
Embroidery hoop
Tapestry needle

INSTRUCTIONS

Before beginning, see the general information on pages 180–183 for special cross-stitch tips and techniques, and for materials necessary for working all counted cross-stitch projects.

Referring to pattern, *above,* chart design on graph paper.

With marking pen, trace outline of bib pattern piece onto hardanger. (*Note:* If apron bib is too narrow for design as shown, substitute a piece of even-weave fabric with a different thread count.) Use three plies of floss and work the cross-stitches over two threads of fabric. Center motif on hardanger, positioning top of motif approximately 1½ inches from top.

Following pattern envelope instructions, complete apron, adding piping and ruffles as desired.

Afghan

Shown on page 21.
Finished size is 51x74 inches.

MATERIALS

Unger Roly Poly yarn (3.5-ounce skeins): 14 skeins white (8001) and 1 skein *each* of bronze (8320), dark green (8729), blue (4556), and yellow (8825)
Paternayan 3-ply Persian yarn (32-

inch lengths): 45 strands *each* of leaf green (632) and yellow-orange (770); 35 strands *each* of pale blue (554), green (630), and yellow (772); 20 strands *each* of blue (553) and blue-green (662); 15 strands of dark blue (550); 10 strands of brown (431); and 5 strands of bronze (750)
Size H afghan crochet hook, or hook size to obtain gauge given below
Size H aluminum crochet hook, or size to obtain gauge given below
Yarn needle

Gauge: With afghan hook, 4 sts = 1 inch; 4 rows = 1 inch. With crochet hook, 4 sc = 1 inch.

INSTRUCTIONS

Use the following abbreviations to crochet this afghan:

ch .... chain
lp(s) .... loop(s)
rem .... remains, remaining
rep .... repeat
rnd(s) .... round(s)
sc .... single crochet
yo .... yarn over
* .... repeat from * as indicated

Note: Each complete row of afghan stitch consists of two parts—the first half of the row and the second half of the row.

With afghan hook and white yarn, ch 194.

First half of Row 1: Retaining all lps on hook, skip first ch, * insert hook in next ch, yo, draw up lp; rep from * across row—194 lps on hook. *Second half of Row 1:* Yo and draw through first lp on hook, * yo, draw through next 2 lps on hook; rep from * until 1 lp rem on hook.

First half of Row 2: Insert hook under *second* vertical bar of previous row, yo, draw up lp and leave on hook; * insert hook under next vertical bar, yo, draw up lp and leave on hook; rep from * to within one bar of end; insert hook under last bar, yo, draw up lp—194 lps. *Second half of Row 2:* Rep second half of Row 1.

Rep both halves of Row 2 until 240 rows have been completed. Insert hook under second vertical bar of previous row, yo, draw lp through vertical bar and lp on hook, * insert hook under next vertical bar, yo, draw lp through vertical bar and lp on hook; rep from * across. Break off yarn and draw tail through rem lp on hook. Fasten off.

BORDER: Using white yarn and with right side facing, work 1 rnd sc in each st and row around, making (sc, ch 2, sc) in each corner; turn. With wrong side facing, work 1 rnd sc around, working corners as before; turn. With right side facing, join bronze and work 1 rnd sc. Continue in this manner, turning work and working in the following color sequence: 1 rnd white, 1 rnd blue, 1 rnd white, 1 rnd green, 1 rnd white, 1 rnd yellow, 2 rnds white. Block afghan according to yarn manufacturer's instructions.

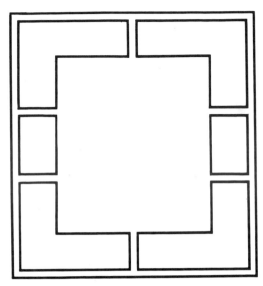

CROSS-STITCH EMBROIDERY: Referring to the border pattern for the sampler, pages 24–29, chart corner and adjacent straight black-eyed susan and bluebell motifs on graph paper.

Chart entire afghan before stitching. Referring to the drawing, *above,* chart corner and straight motifs as shown. At the corners allow 3 rows below bottom motif, 4 rows above top motif, and 4 stitches each side of motif. Leave one stitch between each motif.

Use two plies of Persian yarn and work each cross-stitch over one afghan stitch.

Steam-press embroidery on wrong side.

Prairie Rose Tea Cozy

Shown on page 19.
Finished size is 11½x10¼ inches.

MATERIALS
14x14-inch piece of black hardanger
DMC embroidery floss: 2 skeins of medium parrot green (906) and 1 skein *each* of dark lemon yellow (444), dark shell gray (451), seafoam green (562), medium seafoam green (563), medium yellow (743), garnet (816), dark forest green (987), watermelon (3705), medium watermelon (3706), and light watermelon (3708)
Scrap of black fabric
Polyester fleece, cording
Contrasting fabric for piping and lining
Embroidery hoop
Tapestry needle

INSTRUCTIONS
Before beginning, see the general information on pages 180–183 for special cross-stitch tips and techniques, and for materials necessary for working all counted cross-stitch projects.

Referring to the pattern, *opposite,* chart design on graph paper with felt-tip markers.

Use three plies of floss and work the cross-stitches over two threads of hardanger. Mark centers of chart and baste centers of hardanger; use these lines as reference points while stitching. Stitch, substituting dark shell gray (451) for black. (*Note:* If another fabric color is substituted for black, then retain black for cross-stitches.)

Steam-press stitchery on wrong side.

ASSEMBLY: Using tissue paper, make dome-shaped pattern to cover teapot. Cut out two shapes first and tape them together to determine size and shape of tea cozy; dimensions and contours of individual teapots will vary. Experiment with paper patterns until the correct shape is determined before cutting out any fabric.

If desired, after shape of cozy is determined, add random stripes or other stitchery (such as a family name or special date) below rose motifs to fill out shape (see photograph, page 19).

For back of tea cozy, mark outline on black fabric; lay fabric atop fleece.

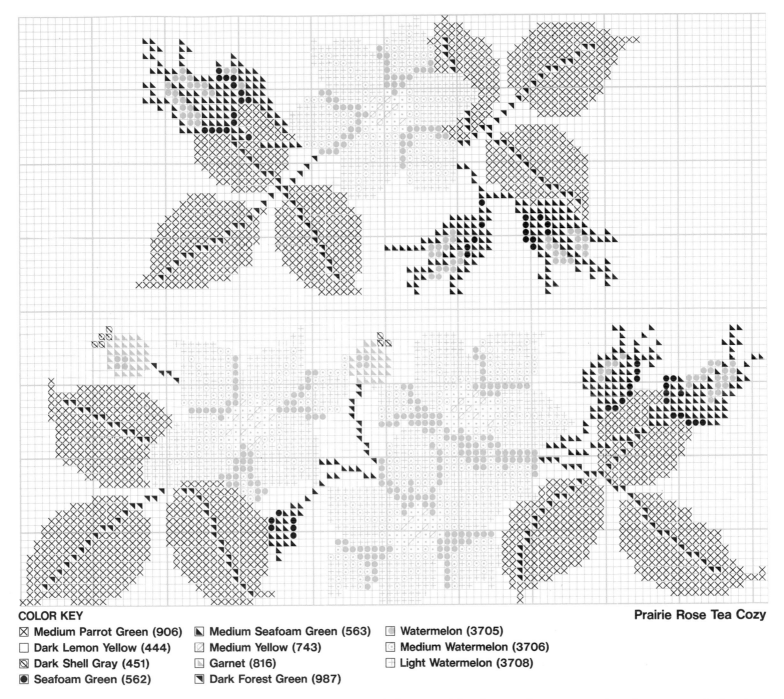

COLOR KEY

⊠ Medium Parrot Green (906) ◣ Medium Seafoam Green (563) ▨ Watermelon (3705)
☐ Dark Lemon Yellow (444) ☑ Medium Yellow (743) ⊡ Medium Watermelon (3706)
⊠ Dark Shell Gray (451) ☐ Garnet (816) ⊟ Light Watermelon (3708)
◉ Seafoam Green (562) ◥ Dark Forest Green (987)

Prairie Rose Tea Cozy

Machine-quilt fabric to fleece in rows of stitching 1 inch apart. Machine-stitch cozy outline on back assembly.

Cover cord to make piping (see general directions, pages 186–187) and loop. Machine-stitch piping to front along outline, adding loop of fabric-covered cord at center top. With right sides facing, stitch front and back together along outline, leaving bottom open. Trim seams to ¼ inch past stitching; clip curves.

Turn cozy; stitch piping along bottom edge. Turn inside out once more.

For lining, cut two cozy shapes from contrasting fabric. With right sides facing, stitch along rounded edge, leaving a 6-inch opening for turning and leaving bottom open.

With right sides facing, stitch raw edges along bottom together. Turn through opening in lining; slip-stitch lining closed. Smooth lining into cozy; tack in several places to secure.

33

Prairie Rose Napkin Caddies

Shown on page 19.
Finished size is 6¼x4⅜ inches.

MATERIALS
For each caddy
14x5-inch piece of white hardanger
DMC embroidery floss: 1 skein *each*
of dark lemon yellow (444),
seafoam green (562), medium
seafoam green (563), medium
yellow (743), medium parrot green
(906), dark forest green (987),
watermelon (3705), medium
watermelon (3706), and light
watermelon (3708)
Fabric for caddy lining and piping
Polyester fleece
String for piping
Embroidery hoop
Tapestry needle

For each napkin
17x17-inch square of fabric

INSTRUCTIONS
Before beginning, see the general information on pages 180–183 for special cross-stitch tips and techniques, and for materials necessary for working all counted cross-stitch projects.

Referring to the pattern for Prairie Rose Tea Cozy, page 33, chart single prairie rose motif (upper motif) on graph paper.

Use three plies of floss and work the cross-stitches over two threads of fabric. Stitch motif in center of strip of hardanger.

Steam-press the stitchery on the wrong side.

ASSEMBLY: Lay stitchery atop fleece. Baste lines along long edge of hardanger ⅜ inch past stitching.

Cover string with fabric to make piping (see general directions, pages 186–187). Sew piping to basted lines.

Cut lining fabric to match hardanger. Press short ends under ½ inch (to wrong side).

With right sides together, sew hardanger to lining along piping lines. Trim away fleece seam allowance and remaining seam allowance to ¼ inch. Turn and press. With right sides of hardanger facing, sew center back seam of caddy. Trim seam allowance. Tuck ends of piping under lining and slip-stitch ends of lining together.

Make 16x16-inch-square napkins from contrasting fabric.

Prairie Rose Blanket Edging

Shown on page 18.
Finished depth of edging is 5¼ inches.

MATERIALS
Woven blanket
8-inch-wide strip of black hardanger;
length of hardanger depends on
size of blanket (see Instructions,
below)
DMC embroidery floss: See
instructions for Prairie Rose Tea
Cozy, page 32, for colors; amounts
will vary with length of edging
Contrasting fabric and cord for piping
Black fabric to line edging
Embroidery hoop
Tapestry needle

INSTRUCTIONS
Before beginning, see the general information on pages 180–183 for special cross-stitch tips and techniques, and for materials necessary for working all counted cross-stitch projects.

Referring to the pattern for Prairie Rose Tea Cozy, chart single bloom motif and three-bloom rose motifs from Prairie Rose Tea Cozy. Mark vertical center of each pattern. Using width of blanket as a guide, position motifs evenly across hardanger strip. Alternate small and large motif to use the width of the blanket to its best advantage.

Baste a centerline along length of hardanger strip. Using this as a reference point, stitch the rose motifs along strip. Use three plies of floss and work the cross-stitches over two threads of fabric.

Steam-press the stitchery on the wrong side.

ASSEMBLY: Trim hardanger to 1½ inches past stitchery along top and bottom; this includes ½-inch seam allowances. Mark length of strip to fit finished width of blanket.

Cover cord with fabric to make piping (see general directions, pages 186–187) to edge top and bottom of stitchery. Cut (and piece, if necessary) backing fabric to same size as edging. Fold under one long edge of backing ½ inch; press.

Stitch piping to front of edging along seam lines. With right sides of edging and blanket facing, stitch together along piping line. Fold up and press. With right sides facing, stitch backing to stitchery along top seam line. Sew short ends of edging and backing closed. Trim seams; clip corners. Turn edging; blindstitch folded-under edge of backing to blanket.

Strawberry Pillow

Shown on page 23.
Finished size is 18x15 inches,
including ruffle.

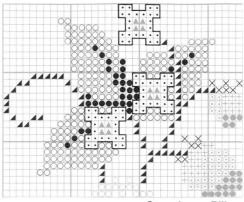

Strawberry Pillow

COLOR KEY

◫ **Deep Parrot Green (904)**
⊡ **White**
⊠ **Dark Shell Gray (451)**
◪ **Light Violet (554)**
◉ **Seafoam Green (562)**
▢ **Light Old Gold (676)**
◮ **Light Tangerine (742)**
⊠ **Medium Parrot Green (906)**
◨ **Watermelon (3705)**
◨ **Medium Watermelon (3706)**
⊞ **Light Watermelon (3708)**

MATERIALS

19x16-inch piece of white hardanger
DMC embroidery floss: 2 skeins of
    deep parrot green (904) and 1
    skein *each* of white, dark shell
    gray (451), light violet (554),
    seafoam green (562), light old gold
    (676), light tangerine (742), medium
    parrot green (906), watermelon
    (3705), medium watermelon (3706),
    and light watermelon (3708).
Fabric for backing, piping, and ruffle
Polyester fiberfill
Embroidery hoop
Tapestry needle

INSTRUCTIONS

Before beginning, see the general information on pages 180–183 for special cross-stitch tips and techniques, and for materials necessary for working all counted cross-stitch projects.

Referring to the pattern, *above,* chart strawberry motif. Reverse pattern and chart its mirror image.

Use three plies of floss and work the cross-stitches over two threads of hardanger. Outline all of the white blooms with backstitches worked in dark shell gray (451).

Measure 3½ inches down and 3½ inches in from the left edge and stitch upper-left strawberry motif (with strawberries on right-hand side) here. Work next two motifs to the right, leaving four stitches between motifs and aligning them at top and bottom; these three motifs form the top row. Work second row of motifs, again leaving four stitches between motifs, *and* reversing center motif so that the strawberries are on the left-hand side. Work the third row of strawberries as for the first.

Measure out 1½ inches past cross-stitching and baste lines for finished size of pillow.

Steam-press the stitchery on the wrong side.

See general directions, pages 186–187, for completing a pillow.

Thistle Mirror Frame

Shown on page 22.
Finished size of stitched area is
7⅝x9⅜ inches.

MATERIALS

13x16-inch piece of cream 14-count
    Aida cloth
DMC embroidery floss: 2 skeins of
    forest green (989) and 1 skein *each*
    of deep violet (550), dark violet
    (552), light violet (554), dark forest
    green (987), and aquamarine (992)
Polyester fleece, muslin
Fabric and cord for piping
Mirror, frame
Embroidery hoop
Tapestry needle

INSTRUCTIONS

Before beginning, see the general information on pages 180–183 for special cross-stitch tips and techniques, and for materials necessary for working all counted cross-stitch projects.

Referring to the pattern for the sampler, pages 24–29, chart thistle motif.

Use three plies of floss and work the cross-stitches over one thread.

To duplicate mirror as shown, measure 3 inches down and 3 inches in from left side. Stitch upper-left thistle motif here. Work three more motifs to the right, leaving three stitches between each one, and aligning them at top and bottom.

For side of frame, work a vertical row of three thistles directly beneath left-hand and right-hand thistle, leaving five stitches between each one, and aligning them at right and left.

For bottom of frame, work a row of four thistles as for top.

Mark a 3¼x6½-inch rectangle in center of motifs for cutout opening.

Steam-press the stitchery on the wrong side.

ASSEMBLY: Cover cord for piping (See general directions, pages 186–187.) Stitch piping to cutout line with raw edges to inside.

Layer stitchery faceup atop fleece. Stitch along cutout line. Pin right side of stitchery to muslin. With fleece side up, stitch along cutout line once more.

Press muslin away from stitchery. Stay-stitch through all thicknesses of seam allowance, pivoting at corners. Cut out all layers of cutout to ⅜ inch from stay stitching. Clip corners. Pull backing fabric through cutout to back; press. Topstitch through all layers along outer edge of stitchery.

Position stitchery atop mirror and frame as desired.

Stitcheries for Family Celebrations

A loving way to record the landmarks in the lives of family and friends is to create a cross-stitch keepsake. This chapter contains projects to commemorate extra-special happenings—a wedding, an anniversary, the birth of a baby, and a move to a new home.

This delicate sampler, *opposite,* is sure to become a treasure for the couple it's stitched for. The traditional cross-stitch sampler motifs—an alphabet and numerals—are updated with the use of a fresh color scheme and sweet heart, flower, and cottage motifs.

Keep in mind that wedding samplers, like the one shown here, make cherished gifts for anniversaries, too. This design records the names, the place, and the date.

Instructions and charts for all the projects in this chapter begin on page 44.

Heart-shaped party favors, such as those pictured *opposite* and at *right*, can be put to several uses at a golden or silver wedding anniversary celebration.

The background material for each heart is perforated paper. The hearts are cut out after the stitching is completed; no further finishing is required.

Cross-stitches worked with metallic thread add touches of sparkle, and the metallic accents can be adapted to a silver or gold color scheme. These two versions are stitched with pink and blue flowers, but you can change the predominant colors of the blossoms to coordinate with any party color scheme.

Use the hearts as shown here for package tie-ons, as accents for any type of flower arrangement, or to trim table accessories. Stitch the motifs on guest book and photo album covers or as the focal point of a special centerpiece.

a day of joy,
november 1, 199▢
a lifetime of love
mindy beth

Most cross-stitchers at one time or another choose to create a stitchery for a new baby. Here are two designs that are as straightforward as they are charming.

The framed wall hanging, *opposite,* is based on the heartfelt sentiment "A day of joy, a lifetime of love." The two remaining lines are for the child's name and birth date. Simple repeat patterns of hearts, flowers, and stripes complete the design. Because of its simplicity, this stitchery is ideal for beginners.

The ruffled pillow, *above,* is based on a similarly simple approach. Rows of pastel stripes combine with rows of hearts and a single repeated word, "JOY!"

With either design, change the four lines of words to convey any greeting, a baby's birth weight and length, or a short poem. See pages 184 and 185 for more on creating original cross-stitch designs from these basic patterns.

Adding a surname or an address to a housewarming present ensures that the whole family will enjoy it. These two lively stitcheries are designed with new households in mind.

The trivet, *above,* can accommodate a last name with as many as 11 or 12 letters, as well as a street address. This round design is suitable for a wooden tray or trivet with an 8-inch-diameter opening and a glass insert. Paint the wooden rim in a color to match the stitchery.

The design for the family name sampler, *opposite,* combines traditional motifs, a vibrant color scheme, and an unusual assortment of alphabets. It's a spectacular focal point for a new home's entry, dining room, or family room.

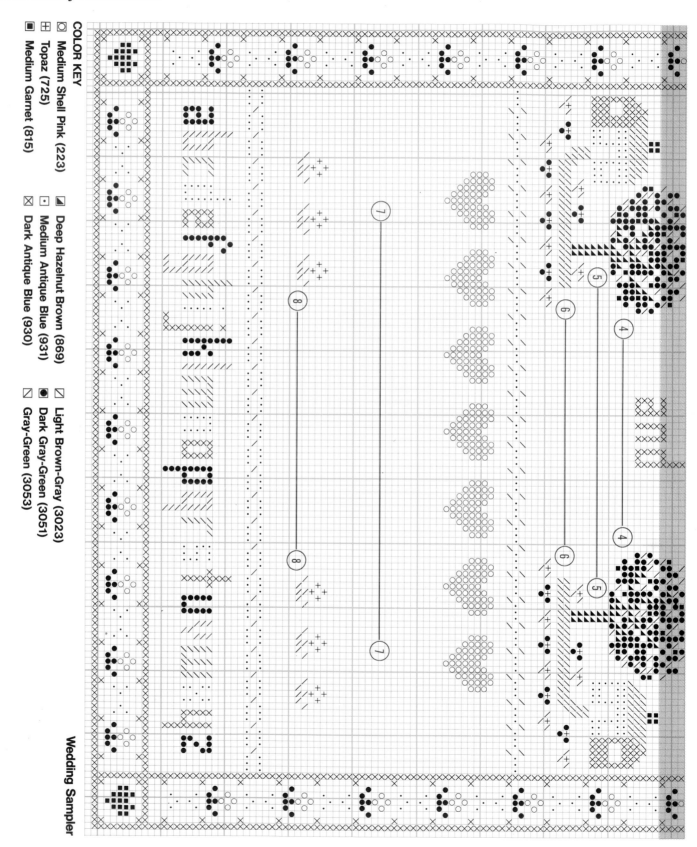

COLOR KEY

◇ Medium Shell Pink (223)
⊞ Topaz (725)
▣ Medium Garnet (815)

◤ Deep Hazelnut Brown (869)
⊡ Medium Antique Blue (931)
⊠ Dark Antique Blue (930)

◩ Light Brown-Gray (3023)
◉ Dark Gray-Green (3051)
◻ Gray-Green (3053)

Wedding Sampler

44

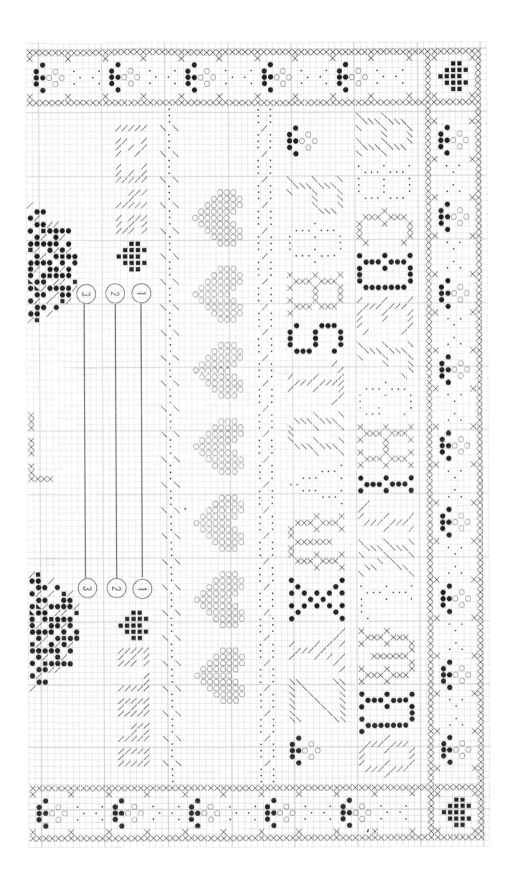

Wedding Sampler

Shown on page 37.
Finished size of stitchery is 5⅜x6⅞ inches.
Design is 125x161 stitches.

MATERIALS

13x15-inch piece of ecru hardanger
DMC embroidery floss: 1 skein each of medium shell pink (223), topaz (725), medium garnet (815), deep hazelnut brown (869), dark antique blue (930), medium antique blue (931), light brown-gray (3023), dark gray-green (3051), and gray-green (3053)
Embroidery hoop
Tapestry needle

INSTRUCTIONS

Before beginning, see the general information on pages 180–183 for special cross-stitch tips and techniques, and for materials necessary for working all counted cross-stitch projects.

Referring to pattern, *left,* chart design onto graph paper using felt-tip markers. To personalize sampler, chart names to be stitched on a separate piece of graph paper, using capital letters from top two rows of sampler pattern and lowercase letters from bottom row of sampler pattern. Also chart the name of the church (or the name of the town where the wedding was held) and the date of the ceremony in lowercase letters.

Transfer words to pattern, centering each line horizontally. For top name, align top of capital letter with Line 1, top of lowercase letter with Line 2, and bottom of all letters with Line 3. For bottom name, align top of capital letter with Line 4, top of lowercase letter with Line 5, and bottom of all letters with Line 6. Align bottom of church or town letters with Line 7.

Align bottom of date letters with Line 8, eliminating yellow flowers on either side of date line for longer dates.

Stitch, using one ply of floss and working the cross-stitches over one thread of hardanger.

Measure 4 inches down from the top and 4 inches in from left side; begin stitching upper-left corner of border here. Fill in alphabets and motifs. Stitch names, place, and date in dark antique blue (930).

Frame the sampler as desired.

Anniversary Heart Favors

Shown on pages 38–39.
Finished size is 3⅜x3⅛ inches.
Design is 49x45 stitches.

MATERIALS
For blue and silver favor
Susan Bates Anchor embroidery
  floss: 1 skein *each* of light blue
  (128), medium blue (130), light
  spruce green (206), spruce green
  (209), and light yellow (292)
Susan Bates Anchor metallic thread:
  1 spool of silver

For pink and gold favor
Susan Bates Anchor embroidery
  floss: 1 skein *each* of medium pink
  (50), light pink (52), light spruce
  green (206), spruce green (209),
  and light yellow (292)
Susan Bates Anchor metallic thread:
  1 spool of gold

For either favor
5x5-inch piece of white perforated
  paper
Tapestry needle

INSTRUCTIONS
Before beginning, see the general information on pages 180–183 for special cross-stitch tips and techniques, and for materials necessary for working all counted cross-stitch projects.

Note that the materials list above designates two separate color combinations, each using a different metallic thread for a specific anniversary. Change color of flower petals, selecting a light and a medium shade to match table linens or color of other accessories.

Referring to pattern, *below,* chart heart motif on graph paper. Mark horizontal and vertical centers of chart. Lightly mark horizontal and vertical centers of perforated paper. Using these lines as reference points, stitch design. Stitch, using two plies of floss and working the design over one space of the paper.

Work vines at upper left and lower right within heart in spruce green (209) backstitches. Outline outer edges of leaves in spruce green (209). Outline flower center and each petal with metallic thread.

Following outline on pattern, cut out heart shape one space beyond stitched outline. Use small, sharp scissors and cut out heart shape from per-

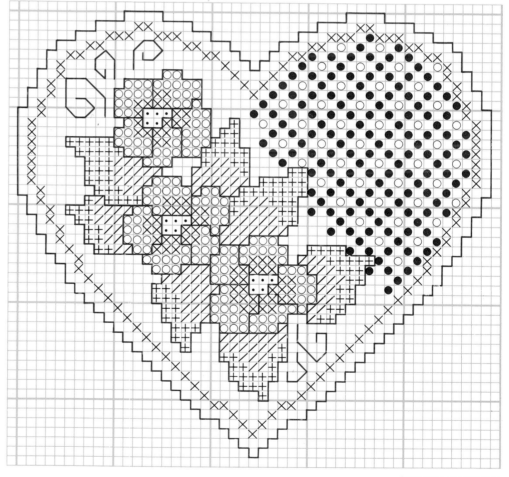

Anniversary Favors

COLOR KEY

▢	Light Blue (128) or Light Pink (52)	◪	Spruce Green (209)
☒	Medium Blue (130) or Medium Pink (50)	⊡	Light Yellow (292)
⊞	Light Spruce Green (206)	◉	Metallic Gold or Metallic Silver

forated paper at right angles from hole to hole.

Note: The basic pattern for the heart favor may be adapted for a variety of uses. For a sachet, stitch the heart onto a scrap of white even-weave fabric, stuff with scented filling (following general directions on pages 186–187), and trim with lace. Follow the same steps to create a Christmas tree ornament; substitute darker, richer colors for the pastel petals and leaves, if desired.

Also consider using the pattern to embellish a guest book or photograph album. Select a suitable fabric to cover the front of the book or album. Design the cover around the heart pattern, incorporating names, dates, or other words into the overall design. For more about creating cross-stitch designs, see pages 184–185.

Birth Announcement Wall Hanging

Shown on page 40.
Finished size is 12¼x11½ inches.
Design is 110x100 stitches.

MATERIALS
20x20-inch piece of 18-count even-weave fabric
Susan Bates Anchor embroidery floss: 1 skein *each* of green (261), dark green (262), yellow (297), pink (74), medium blue (978), and dark blue (979)
Embroidery hoop
Tapestry needle

INSTRUCTIONS
Before beginning, see the general information on pages 180–183 for special cross-stitch tips and techniques, and for materials necessary for working all counted cross-stitch projects.

Referring to pattern for wall hanging, page 48, chart upper and lower border designs on graph paper, leaving center space open for greeting.

For lettering, use alphabet shown on patterns for Birth Announcement Wall Hanging, page 48 (lines 2 and 4), and Birth Announcement Pillow, page 49 (lines 1 and 4), to chart birth date and name to complete the following:

a day of joy (for Line 1)
baby's birth date (for Line 2)
a lifetime of love (for Line 3)
baby's name (for Line 4)

Chart baby's birth date and name on separate pieces of graph paper. Find center of each line and transfer both lines to the master pattern as indicated above, centering each left and right. Align bottom of letters with the lines indicated on pattern

Stitch, using four plies of floss and working the cross-stitches over two threads of fabric.

Measure 4 inches down from the top and 4 inches in from the left; begin stitching upper-left corner of border here. Stitch upper design first. Baste four lines for greeting; stitch greeting, working baby's name in dark blue (979). Stitch lower design.

Steam-press the stitchery on the wrong side. Frame as desired.

Birth Announcement Pillow

Shown on page 41.
Finished size is 19x19 inches, including ruffle.
Design is 110x110 stitches.

MATERIALS
20x20-inch piece of 18-count even-weave fabric
Susan Bates Anchor embroidery floss: 1 skein *each* of green (261), dark green (262), yellow (297), pink (74), light blue (977), medium blue (978), and dark blue (979)
Fabric for border, backing, and ruffle
Polyester fiberfill
Embroidery hoop, tapestry needle

INSTRUCTIONS
Before beginning, see the general information on pages 180–183 for special cross-stitch tips and techniques, and for materials necessary for working all counted cross-stitch projects.

Referring to pattern for pillow, page 49, chart design on graph paper.

For lettering, use alphabet shown on patterns for Birth Announcement Wall Hanging, page 48, and Birth Announcement Pillow, page 49, to chart baby's birth date and baby's name to complete the following:

baby's name (for Line 1)
joined our family (for Line 2)
on this day (for Line 3)
baby's birth date (for Line 4)

Chart baby's birth date and name on separate pieces of graph paper. Find center of each line and transfer both lines to the master pattern as indicated above, centering each left and right. Align bottom of letters with the lines indicated on pattern.

Stitch, using four plies of floss and working the cross-stitches over two threads of fabric.

Measure 4 inches down from the top and 4 inches in from the left; begin stitching upper-left corner of border here. Stitch upper design first, then add greeting and lower border.

Steam-press the stitchery on the wrong side.

Refer to directions on pages 186–187 to complete pillow.

a day of joy,

stuvwxyz

a lifetime of love,

1234567890,

COLOR KEY

- ◉ Green (261)
- ◢ Dark Green (262)
- ⊞ Yellow (297)
- ⊡ Pink (74)
- ○ Medium Blue (978)

Birth Announcement Wall Hanging

Birth Announcement Pillow

COLOR KEY

- ◉ Green (261)
- ◢ Dark Green (262)
- ⊞ Yellow (297)
- ⊡ Pink (74)
- ◺ Light Blue (977)
- ◩ Medium Blue (978)
- ⊠ Dark Blue (979)

49

COLOR KEY

◤ ◣ Christmas Red (304)

◨ ⊠ Dark Hunter Green (3345)

☐ ◿ Rose (335)

■ ◼ Dark Steel Gray (414)

⊞ Pale Yellow (744)

◉ ● Deep Pistachio Green (890)

▣ ⊡ Dark Antique Blue (930)

◻ ◿ Light Antique Blue (932)

⊞ Ⅰ Medium Dusty Rose (962)

⊡ · Light Loden Green (3364)

Housewarming Sampler

50

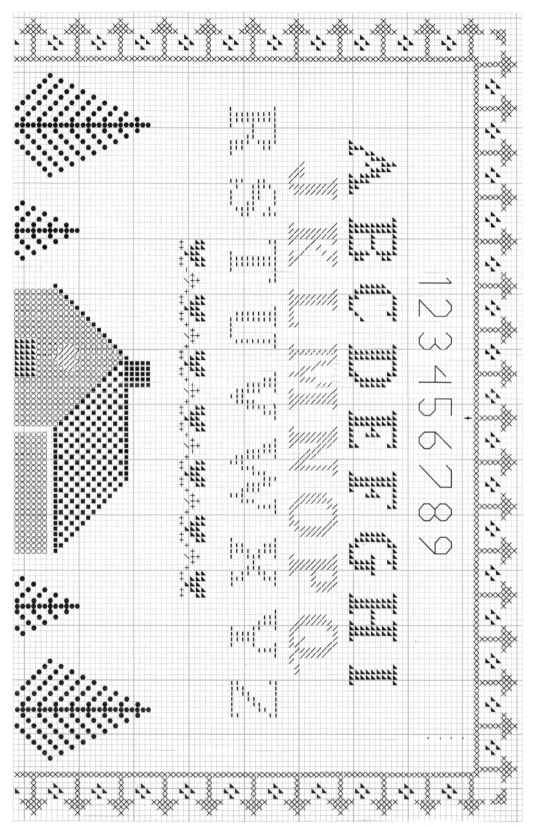

Housewarming Sampler

Shown on page 43.
Finished size is 12x17 inches.
Design is 145x201 stitches.

MATERIALS
22x27-inch piece of white 11-count
 Aida cloth
DMC embroidery floss: 2 skeins *each*
 of medium Christmas red (304)
 and dark hunter green (3345) and
 1 skein *each* of rose (335), dark
 steel gray (414), pale yellow (744),
 deep pistachio green (890), dark
 antique blue (930), light antique
 blue (932), medium dusty rose
 (962), and light loden green (3364)
Embroidery hoop
Tapestry needle

INSTRUCTIONS
 Before beginning, see the general information on pages 180–183 for special cross-stitch tips and techniques,
and for materials necessary for working all counted cross-stitch projects.
 Referring to pattern, *left,* chart design on graph paper. Referring to alphabet chart, page 72, chart family
name on a separate piece of graph
paper. Transfer name to master graph,
centering it left and right, and aligning
top of letters with Line 1 and bottom
of letters with Line 2.
 Stitch, using four plies of floss and
working the cross-stitches over one
thread of fabric.
 Measure 5 inches down from top of
fabric and 5 inches in from the left
side; begin stitching upper-left corner
of border here.
 Make a French knot using four plies
of pale yellow (744) in the center of
each of the four-stitch clusters of medium Christmas red (304), around border and above family name.

COLOR KEY

⊡	Light Blue (160)	◢ Dark Green (263)
⊞	Light Green (261)	◯ Yellow (302)

⊟ Medium Turquoise (779)   ⊠ Gray (900)

⊡ Dark Turquoise (851)   ⧅ Medium Mauve (970)   ◉ Dark Mauve (972)

Work numerals across top of sampler and stems and leaves in backstitches using light loden green (3364). Add French knot blossoms atop stems using various colors. Make doorknob with French knot using dark steel gray (414). Add stitcher's name and date to sampler if desired.

Trivet

Shown on page 42.
Finished diameter of stitchery is 8 inches.
Design is 111x113 stitches.

MATERIALS
12x12-inch piece of white 14-count Aida cloth
Susan Bates Anchor embroidery floss: 1 skein *each* of light blue (160), light green (261), dark green (263), yellow (302), medium turquoise (779), dark turquoise (851), gray (900), medium mauve (970), and dark mauve (972)
Wooden trivet designed to receive 8-inch-diameter stitchery inset
Embroidery hoop
Tapestry needle

INSTRUCTIONS
Before beginning, see the general information on pages 180–183 for special cross-stitch tips and techniques, and for materials necessary for working all counted cross-stitch projects.

Referring to pattern, *opposite,* chart design. On a separate piece of graph paper, chart surname, using alphabet from Housewarming Sampler (pattern is on pages 50–51). Chart street address using alphabet, *right.* Transfer name and address to master pattern.

Stitch, using two plies of floss and working the cross-stitches over one thread of fabric.

Steam-press stitchery on wrong side and insert in trivet.

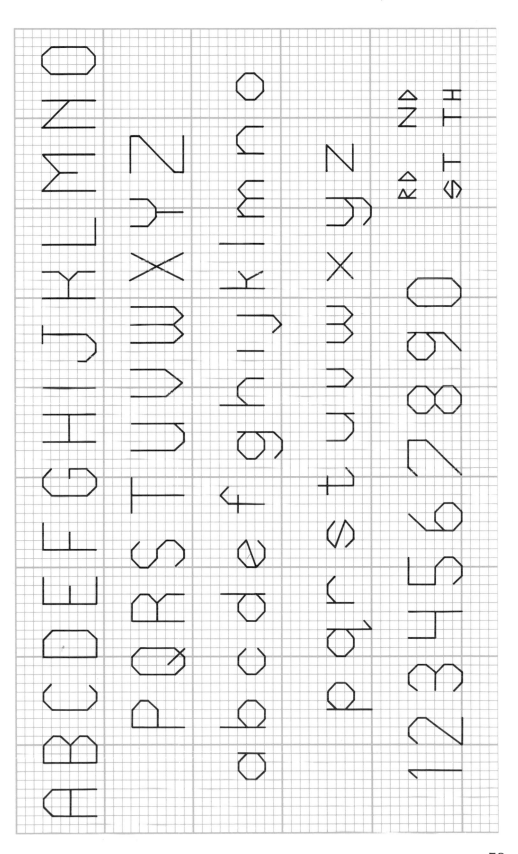

Cherries For a Country Kitchen

Count on these sprightly cherry motifs to liven up a kitchen. Use them to decorate table linens, to edge a set of shelf liners, and to accent a pair of picture frames. The accompanying sampler is based on a 1930s-style alphabet.

This collection of cherry designs is tailor-made for a country kitchen.

Design one or more shelf liners like the one shown here for any size cupboard. Borders of piping and eyelet trims add a homey touch.

A black background adds dramatic impact to the sampler *opposite*.

Instructions begin on page 58.

T wo cheerful cherry motifs brighten the place mats and napkins *opposite* and assure an inviting table setting. The place mats feature larger motifs in two corners, and the napkins are decorated with smaller cherries bordered by checks. Design the borders for the picture mats, *above*, to accommodate any size frame. These motifs are borrowed from the sampler on page 55 and from the napkins, *opposite*.

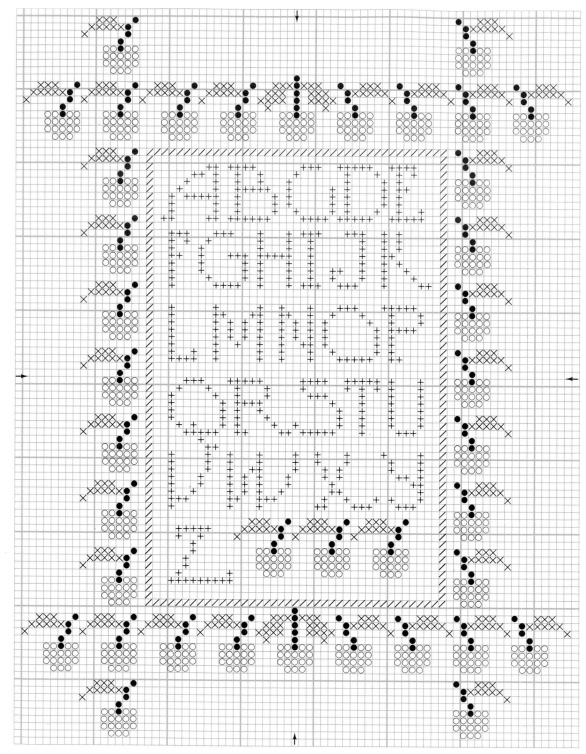

COLOR KEY

◉ Deep Mahogany (300)
◻ Christmas Red (321)
⊞ Light Coral (352)
⊠ Light Christmas Green (701)
▨ Pale Delft (800)

Sampler

Sampler

Shown on page 55.
Finished size is 5½x7 inches.
Stitchery is 85 stitches wide and 98 stitches high.

MATERIALS

18x20-inch piece of black 14-count Aida cloth
DMC embroidery floss: 1 skein *each* of deep mahogany (300), Christmas red (321), light coral (352), light Christmas green (701), and pale delft (800)
Embroidery hoop
Tapestry needle

INSTRUCTIONS

Before beginning, see the general information on pages 180–183 for special cross-stitch tips and techniques, and for materials necessary for working all counted cross-stitch projects.

Referring to pattern, *opposite,* chart design onto graph paper using felt-tip markers.

Use two plies of floss, and work the cross-stitches over one thread of fabric.

Measure 7 inches down from the top and 7 inches in from left side; begin stitching upper-left corner of border here. Mount fabric in hoop and start cross-stitching with outside cherry border. Fill in alphabet and remaining cherry motifs.

Frame the sampler as desired.

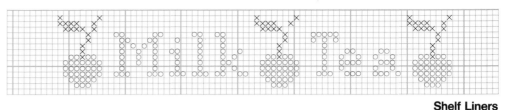
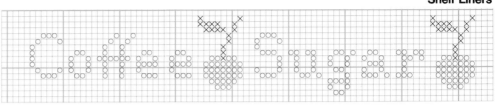

Shelf Liners

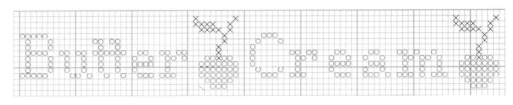

COLOR KEY

◻ **Christmas Red (321)**   ⊠ **Light Christmas Green (701)**

Shelf Liners

Shown on pages 54–55.
Finished size is 6 inches deep, including eyelet ruffle.
Stitchery is 13 stitches high at highest point.

MATERIALS
For each liner
6-inch-wide length of white hardanger as long as shelf plus 1 inch
DMC embroidery floss: 1 skein *each* of Christmas red (321) and light Christmas green (701)
Red piping and white gathered eyelet in same lengths as hardanger
Embroidery hoop, tapestry needle

INSTRUCTIONS

Plan finished width of shelf liner; calculate number of stitches needed to span shelf width by multiplying width in inches by 11. (For example, a 22-inch-wide shelf will accommodate 242 stitches.)

Using patterns, *above,* and graph paper, chart words and cherry motifs so that elements are evenly spaced across liner. Repeat words as shown, or arrange as desired. (*Note:* Begin each additional shelf liner with a different word to avoid a repetitious pattern when all liners are in place.)

Use three plies of floss and work the cross-stitches over two threads of fabric.

Begin stitching at least 1½ inches from left side and 1¾ inches up from bottom edge.

When stitching is completed, machine-zigzag-stitch along bottom edge to prevent raveling. Pin and sew piping and eyelet to bottom edge, right sides facing; open and press raw edges toward top. Stitch ¼-inch hem along top edge and sides.

Press a fold 2 inches below the top edge, wrong sides together. Align this pressed fold with edge of shelf so that stitchery hangs down; secure in place with tacks or double-faced tape.

Place Mats

Shown on page 56.
Finished size is 18½x15¼ inches,
excluding trim.

MATERIALS
For each place mat
24x21-inch piece of white hardanger
DMC embroidery floss: 1 skein *each*
   of Christmas red (321), light
   Christmas green (701), and
   medium garnet (815)
Backing fabric, red jumbo rickrack
Embroidery hoop, tapestry needle

INSTRUCTIONS
Before beginning, see the general information on pages 180–183 for special cross-stitch tips and techniques, and for materials necessary for working all counted cross-stitch projects.

Referring to pattern, *below,* chart design onto graph paper using felt-tip markers.

Use three plies of floss, and work the cross-stitches over two threads of fabric.

Lay out fabric so that 24-inch-long edge is horizontal. Measure 5 inches down from top edge and 5 inches in from left edge; begin stitching upper-left corner of red border here. Work 145 stitches toward right edge to form top border and work a total of 100 stitches down from beginning stitch to form left border.

Work cherry motifs from chart, *left,* in upper-right and lower-left corners of place mats. Then continue red border stitches as indicated until a continuous stitched border is worked around mat, forming a right angle in lower-right corner. See photograph, page 56.

Trim hardanger 2½ inches beyond stitched border. Machine-zigzag-stitch along raw edges to prevent raveling. Cut white backing fabric to same size; place right sides of hardanger and backing together. Pin edges, inserting and centering rickrack along stitching line. Ease rickrack around corners; overlap ends inconspicuously along bottom edge. Using ½-inch seams, stitch around, leaving an opening along bottom edge for turning. Clip corners, turn, press, and slip-stitch opening closed.

Napkins

Shown on page 56.
Finished size is 14x14 inches.
Design is 162x162 stitches.

MATERIALS
For each napkin
16x16-inch piece of white hardanger
DMC embroidery floss: 1 skein *each*
   of Christmas red (321) and light
   Christmas green (701)
Embroidery hoop
Tapestry needle

INSTRUCTIONS
Before beginning, see the general information on pages 180–183 for special cross-stitch tips and techniques, and for materials necessary for working all counted cross-stitch projects.

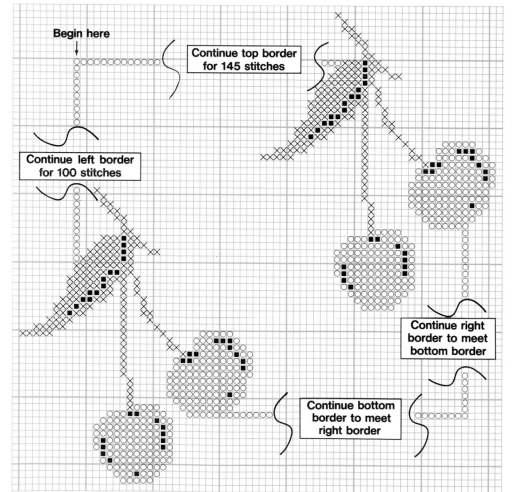

Begin here

Continue top border
for 145 stitches

Continue left border
for 100 stitches

Continue right
border to meet
bottom border

Continue bottom
border to meet
right border

Place Mat

COLOR KEY
▢ Christmas Red (321)   ⊠ Light Christmas Green (701)   ▣ Medium Garnet (815)

Referring to pattern, *below right*, chart design onto graph paper. Pattern shown represents one-fourth of the design. To complete design, turn the pattern one-quarter turn *counterclockwise,* and chart the design directly to the right of the first pattern. Turn the pattern once more and chart the remaining corner directly above the fourth of the pattern just charted. Turn the pattern one final time and chart the remaining corner. The completed napkin pattern will have 16 checks along each edge and four cherries, with the stems of each pointing in a different direction.

Use three plies of floss and work the cross-stitches over two threads of fabric. Stitch napkin. Steam-press on wrong side, and finish edges with a hem about ½ inch past stitching.

Picture Frames

Shown on page 57.

MATERIALS
Scraps of 10-count needlepoint
  canvas or perforated paper
DMC embroidery floss *or* Size 3 pearl
  cotton in colors indicated in
  instructions for sampler, page 59
Picture frames, mat board
Embroidery hoop
Tapestry needle

INSTRUCTIONS
Before beginning, see the general information on pages 180–183 for special cross-stitch tips and techniques, and for materials necessary for working all counted cross-stitch projects.

To plan design, measure inside dimensions of the frame. Then calculate the number of stitches possible for each dimension by multiplying the dimension times the stitch count of the fabric to be used for the frame. For example, an 8x10-inch frame filled with 10-count needlepoint canvas will accommodate 80x100 stitches. A 5x7-inch picture frame will accommodate 70x98 stitches using 14-count perforated paper.

Using the patterns for the sampler, page 58, or napkins, *below,* chart portions of the cherry motifs as desired. The individual cherry motifs from the napkins, spaced with four-stitch checks, are suitable for frame designs. Or use the multiple cherry border from the sampler. Use squares of cross-stitches to fill spaces, if desired.

Stitch the design on the background material desired.

ASSEMBLY: For needlepoint canvas frames, trim canvas to fit within frame; mount on white mat board. Mount photograph on mat board and trim to fit within stitched motifs. Affix photograph to canvas with spray adhesive and secure canvas assembly inside frame.

For perforated paper frames, cut a piece of mat board to fit inside frame. Trim perforated paper to fit frame; cut out center opening. Mount the photograph on the board, positioning the photograph behind the opening.

Layer perforated paper and mat board; secure inside frame.

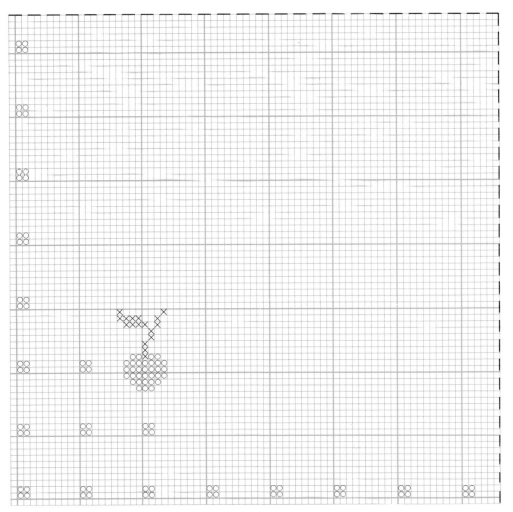

COLOR KEY   **Napkin**
◻ Christmas Red (321)   ⊠ Light Christmas Green (701)

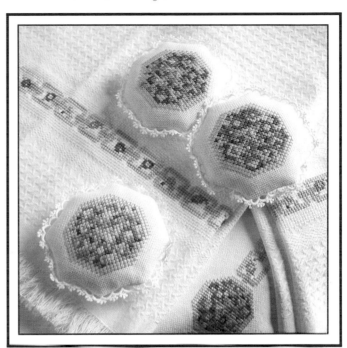

Cross-Stitch For Every Room

Making glorious home accessories is a favorite way for stitchers to display their skills. This chapter features accessories to make for the home, including table coverings and pillows—along with an alphabet to personalize them.

The sumptuous tablecloth, *left,* is an heirloom stitchery that will remain beautiful for decades. In this pattern, sprigs of pastel flowers trim the small links of a golden chain. Larger, octagonal links are filled with an overall flower design. The pattern for each octagon is identical; simply switch the three shades of floss used for the petals.

Portions of the pattern are ideal for smaller projects, *above.* Repeating just the links makes a perfect trim on guest towels. The octagonal motif makes beautiful sachets.

63

The alphabet used for the projects on these two pages is suitable for monogramming many types of accessories.

The old-fashioned candle screen, *above,* is designed to show off your needlework, and is just the right size for an initial (worked over two threads) and a single flower motif (worked over one thread).

The initial pin, *above,* began as a button to cover. Merely slip the stitchery over the button base, secure the backing, and add lace trim and a jewelry pin backing.

Many stores that sell cross-stitch materials carry hand mirrors like the one *above.* Add a stitched monogram to the back, and trim with gold braid and a bow.

B eautiful initials and borders are what make cross-stitched monograms so luxurious. The deeply ruffled pillow shams, *opposite,* are a prime example. The fanciful initial is centered and stitched over three threads. Then it is enhanced with a flower-and-leaf-motif border worked along each side. (The border on the left is simply the reverse of the one on the right.)

As an alternative to these shams, stitch the border and initial across the edge of a pillowcase or center it across the edge of a flat sheet.

Self-contained flower motifs and floral borders designed for cross-stitch are sought after for their versatility. Here are three fresh patterns that will give a springtime lift to any room in your house.

The violet and pansy patterns are made into rectangular pillows, *opposite*. Because they're stitched on even-weave fabric with a large stitch count, the designs work up quickly. The cross-stitching on this pair of pillows can be stitched in a week's worth of evenings.

The remaining design consists of a repeat pattern of yellow roses and trailing violets. It's an ideal design for wrapping around one end of a bolster, *left,* or for stitching on a pair of curtain tiebacks, *above.*

H ere's a truly unusual afghan, *opposite*. The basis for this four-seasons pattern is a specially designed panel of even-weave fabric. It features a rectangular band defined by raised threads. This panel is available at shops that carry cross-stitch fabrics, although it might require a special order.

The rectangle outlines the area of the cross-stitches. One symbol of each of the four seasons is stitched in a corner, then flanked by border motifs that reflect the foliage of the season. For example, a pumpkin keeps company with a garland of frost-tinged oak, alder, and maple leaves.

For a different look, you might embroider just one season's motifs. Work the corner motif four times and the accompanying foliage along each side of the afghan.

Chain-of-Flowers Tablecloth

Shown on pages 62–63.
Finished size is 40¼x40¼ inches.

MATERIALS
44x44-inch piece of white hardanger
DMC embroidery floss: 8 skeins of
  medium yellow (743); 4 skeins
  each of pale avocado green (471)
  and very pale avocado green
  (472); and 2 skeins *each* of
  medium coral (350), light coral
  (352), peach flesh (353), avocado
  green (469), light tangerine (742),
pale yellow (744), dark blue (825),
  medium blue (826), pale blue (827),
  geranium (956), pale geranium
  (957), pale dusty rose (963), dark
  fuchsia (3607), fuchsia (3608), and
  light fuchsia (3609)
Piping and lace for edging
Embroidery hoop
Tapestry needle

INSTRUCTIONS
Before beginning, see the general information on pages 180–183 for special cross-stitch tips and techniques,
and for materials necessary for working all counted cross-stitch projects.

Refer to pattern, *below,* and chart
octagonal motifs and adjacent links.

Measure 3½ inches down from the
top and 3½ inches in from the left on
hardanger square. Begin stitching corner octagon here.

Stitch, using three plies of floss and
working the cross-stitches over two
threads of fabric.

Stitch all yellow chains around
edges of cloth first; fill in centers.
Make a total of nine octagons along
each side, including corner octagons.

Use the same flower pattern for the
center of each octagon, but vary the
three colors used for the petals in
each octagon. Use three shades of
pink (956, 957, and 963) for the corners. Then, working toward the right
from a corner, stitch the flowers in the

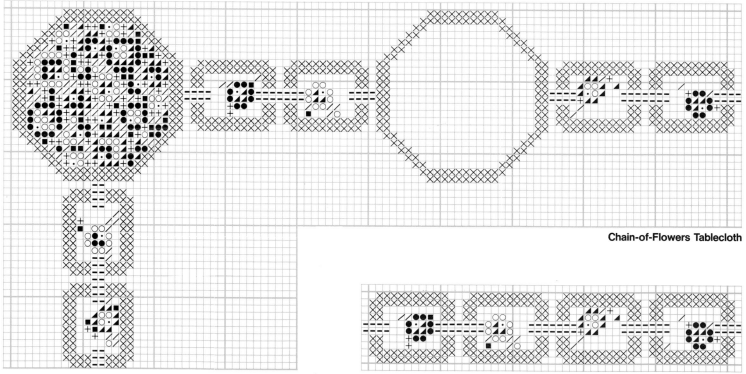

Chain-of-Flowers Tablecloth

Guest Towel Border Design

COLOR KEY
⊟ **Light Tangerine (742)**
⊠ **Medium Yellow (743)**
⊡ **Pale Yellow (744)**
◼ **Avocado Green (469)**
⊞ **Pale Avocado Green (471)**
◿ **Very Pale Avocado Green (472)**

For links with coral flowers:
◉ **Medium Coral (350)**
◿ **Light Coral (352)**
○ **Peach Flesh (353)**

For links with blue flowers:
◉ **Dark Blue (825)**
◿ **Medium Blue (826)**
○ **Pale Blue (827)**

For links with rose flowers:
◉ **Geranium (956)**
◿ **Pale Geranium (957)**
○ **Pale Dusty Rose (963)**

For links with fuchsia flowers:
◉ **Dark Fuchsia (3607)**
◿ **Fuchsia (3608)**
○ **Light Fuchsia (3609)**

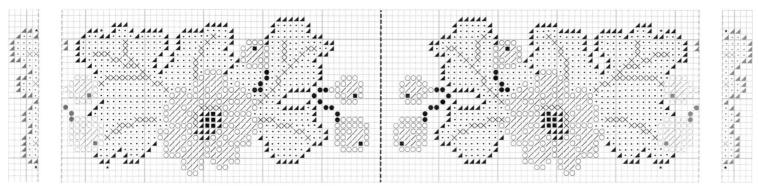

COLOR KEY

⊡ **Light Khaki Green (3013)**   ◪ **Medium Old Gold (729)**   ⊠ **Dark Khaki Green (3011)**   ◼ **Black-Brown (3371)**

◉ **Chocolate (632)**   ⬕ **Light Salmon (761)**   ⊙ **Medium Salmon (3328)**

next octagon in three shades of blue (825, 826, and 827), the next octagon in shades of coral (350, 352, and 353), and the next octagon in shades of fuchsia (3607, 3608, and 3609). Continue in this sequence until all octagons are filled in. Work the small blossoms inside the links in the same shades as the adjacent octagon.

Finish edges with piping and lace.

Octagonal Sachets

Shown on page 63.
Finished size is 4x4 inches.
Design is 24x24 stitches.

MATERIALS
For a set of four sachets
12x12-inch piece of white Davosa fabric
DMC embroidery floss: 1 skein *each* of the colors required for the Chain-of-Flowers Tablecloth; see materials list, page 70. *Note:* Design does not call for light tangerine (742).
Fabric scraps for backing
Potpourri, 60 inches of white lace
Embroidery hoop, tapestry needle

INSTRUCTIONS
Before beginning, see the general information on pages 180–183 for special cross-stitch tips and techniques, and for materials necessary for working all counted cross-stitch projects.

Referring to pattern, *opposite,* for Chain-of-Flowers Tablecloth, chart just the octagonal motif.

Cut four 6x6-inch squares of Davosa fabric. Stitch, using four plies of floss and working the cross-stitches over two threads of fabric.

Stitch octagon first. Then fill in center with flower designs, using a different set of three shades for the petals. See the directions for Chain-of-Flowers Tablecloth for each variation.

Steam-press the stitcheries on the wrong side.

Mark stitching line ⅝ inch beyond stitched octagon. See pages 186–187 for completing an ornament; trim with lace and fill with potpourri.

Towels

Shown on page 63.
Design is 10 stitches high.

MATERIALS
Victoria woven towel with even-weave bands (available from Norden Crafts)
DMC embroidery floss: 2 skeins of light tangerine (742); 1 skein of medium yellow (743); and small amounts of remaining colors required for Chain-of-Flowers Tablecloth; see materials list, page 70
Embroidery hoop
Tapestry needle

INSTRUCTIONS
Before beginning, see the general information on pages 180–183 for special cross-stitch tips and techniques, and for materials necessary for working all counted cross-stitch projects.

Chart chain pattern, *opposite,* onto graph paper.

Stitch, using three plies of floss and working the cross-stitches over one thread of the even-weave band.

Center design on band and stitch. Use shades of pink, coral, blue, and fuchsia for blossoms within links.

Repeat chain design on the other end of the towel.

Steam-press the stitchery on the wrong side.

71

Monogrammed Pillow Shams

Shown on page 65.
Finished size is 19x25 inches,
excluding ruffle.
Flower-and-leaf design is
27 stitches high.

MATERIALS
For each sham
22x28-inch piece of white 18-count
   Aida cloth
DMC embroidery floss: 2 skeins of
   light khaki green (3013) and 1
   skein *each* of chocolate (632), ·
medium old gold (729), light
salmon (761), dark khaki green
(3011), medium salmon (3328), and
black-brown (3371)
Fabric for piping, backing, and ruffle
Polyester fleece
Embroidery hoop
Tapestry needle

INSTRUCTIONS
Before beginning, see the general information on pages 180–183 for special cross-stitch tips and techniques, and for materials necessary for working all counted cross-stitch projects.

Referring to alphabet, *below,* chart initial desired. Chart flower-and-leaf design, page 71, with two repeat patterns of each side. To complete ends of repeats, substitute leaf pattern at far left and far right; overlap patterns so that stars align.

Stitch flower-and-leaf design, using four plies of floss and working the cross-stitches over two threads of fabric. Stitch initial, using six plies of floss and working the cross-stitches over three threads of fabric.

Baste a line at vertical center of fabric; baste a second, horizontal line 7½ inches down from top of fabric between the left and right edges. Using light salmon (761) and medium salmon (3328), center and stitch initial at point where basted lines intersect. Skip four threads of Aida cloth at both sides of initial; stitch flower-and-leaf motifs on both sides of initial.

Steam-press on the wrong side.

Trim stitchery to 26x20 inches; line with fleece. For back, cut two 18¼x20-inch fabric pieces. Hem one long edge of each. Overlap pieces, right side up, to make a 26x20-inch rectangle with hemmed edges in the center. Baste together; treat as one piece. Refer to general directions, pages 186–187, to complete sham.

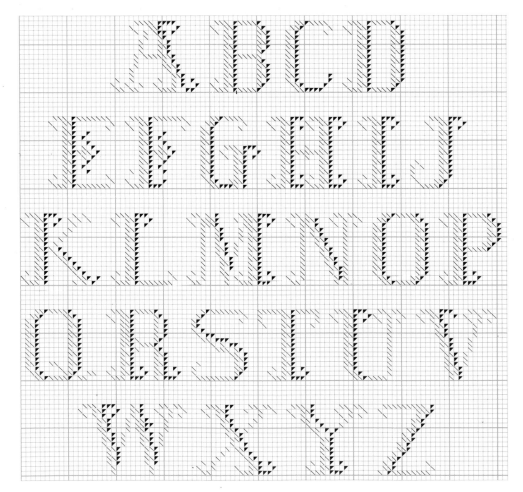

Monogrammed Candle Screen

Shown on page 64.

MATERIALS
Candle screen designed for 3x4-inch
   needlework insert
6x7-inch piece of ecru hardanger
DMC embroidery floss: 1 skein *each*
   of colors used for Pillow Shams;
   see materials list, page 72
Polyester fleece, masking tape
Embroidery hoop
Tapestry needle

INSTRUCTIONS

Before beginning, see the general information on pages 180–183 for special cross-stitch tips and techniques, and for materials necessary for working all counted cross-stitch projects.

Referring to alphabet, *opposite*, chart initial on graph paper. Chart one repeat of flower-and-leaf motif from Monogrammed Pillow Shams; see pattern, page 71. Mark centers.

Using dark khaki green (3011) and light khaki green (3013), stitch initial on fabric. Use three plies of floss and work the cross-stitches over two threads of fabric.

Center and stitch flower-and-leaf motif directly beneath initial, skipping four threads of fabric. Use two plies of floss and work the cross-stitches over one thread of fabric.

Steam-press on the wrong side. Pad with fleece and secure in screen.

Initial Pin

Shown on page 64.
Design is 15 stitches high.

MATERIALS

Scrap of 25-count Lugana linen
Embroidery floss: any two colors
1½-inch-diameter button to cover
Glue-on pin back, lace (optional)
Embroidery hoop, tapestry needle

INSTRUCTIONS

Before beginning, see the general information on pages 180–183 for special cross-stitch tips and techniques, and for materials necessary for working all counted cross-stitch projects.

Referring to alphabet pattern, *opposite*, stitch initial on linen. Use three plies of floss and work the cross-stitches over two threads of fabric.

Remove button shank. Cover button with stitchery. Attach pin back; glue lace to back edge of pin, if desired.

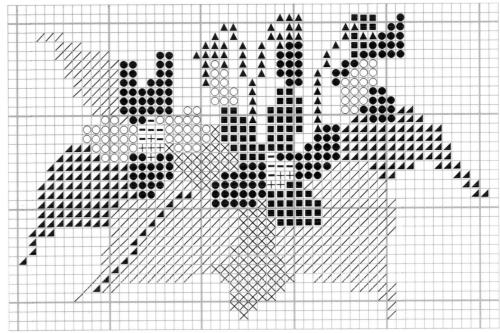

COLOR KEY   Violet Pillow

◉	Deep Lavender (208)	▣	Plum (718)	⊟	Light Pumpkin (970)
◎	Light Lavender (211)	⊞	Pale Topaz (727)	⊠	Dark Hunter Green (3345)
◿	Pale Avocado Green (472)	▲	Light Parrot Green (907)	◿	Light Yellow Green (3348)

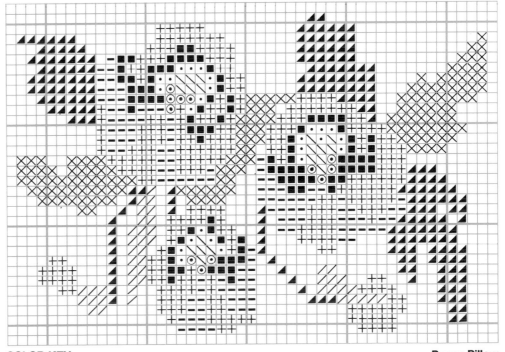

COLOR KEY   Pansy Pillow

◻	White	▣	Plum (718)	⊟	Pumpkin (971)
◉	Medium Coral (350)	⊞	Pale Topaz (727)	⊠	Dark Hunter Green (3345)
◿	Pale Avocado Green (472)	⊡	Deep Cornflower Blue (791)	◿	Light Yellow Green (3348)

Monogrammed Hand Mirror

Shown on page 64.

MATERIALS

8x8-inch piece of ecru Davosa fabric
Embroidery floss: 1 skein *each* of two colors for initial, plus 1 additional skein to complete background
Hand mirror designed to receive needlework insert
Scrap of polyester fleece
Scraps of gold braid and ecru ribbon
Embroidery hoop, tapestry needle

INSTRUCTIONS

Before beginning, see the general information on pages 180–183 for special cross-stitch tips and techniques, and for materials necessary for working all counted cross-stitch projects.

Referring to alphabet, page 72, chart initial desired. Stitch initial in center of fabric piece. Use four plies of floss and work the cross-stitches over two threads.

Mark a circle on fabric that is ¼ inch beyond backing of cardboard insert so that initial is centered.

To create background design, stitch a square tipped on end around initial. Work the sides of the squares in diagonal lines so that each side is made with the same number of stitches. Work a row of stitches directly above the top of square to the circle mark; work a row of stitches directly below bottom of square similarly. Then work rows of stitches in lines parallel to these beginning rows, just past outer circle and leaving two threads of fabric between each row. Fill in the rows between the stitched lines with stitches, leaving every other two threads empty.

Steam-press on the wrong side.

Pad cardboard insert with fleece. Smooth stitchery atop fleece; secure to back of cardboard with tape. Glue insert to back of mirror.

Trim rim of stitchery with gold braid or other trim, overlapping braid slightly at bottom of circle. Add a small ecru bow to conceal ends of braid.

Rectangular Pillows

Shown on page 66.
Finished size is 17x19 inches, including ruffle.
Violet design is 51 stitches wide and 33 stitches high; pansy design is 57 stitches wide and 32 stitches high.

MATERIALS
For violet pillow

DMC embroidery floss: 1 skein *each* of deep lavender (208), light lavender (211), very pale avocado green (472), plum (718), pale topaz (727), light parrot green (907), light pumpkin (970), dark hunter green (3345), and light yellow-green (3348)

For pansy pillow

DMC embroidery floss: 1 skein *each* of white, medium coral (350), very pale avocado green (472), plum (718), pale topaz (727), deep cornflower blue (791), pumpkin (971), dark hunter green (3345), and light yellow-green (3348)

For either pillow

8x11-inch piece of white 14-count Aida cloth
Fabric for borders, piping, and ruffle
Polyester fleece and fiberfill
Embroidery hoop, tapestry needle

INSTRUCTIONS

Before beginning, see the general information on pages 180–183 for special cross-stitch tips and techniques, and for materials necessary for working all counted cross-stitch projects.

Referring to pattern, page 73, chart designs on graph paper. Note horizontal and vertical centers. Baste horizontal and vertical centers of fabric. Using center lines as points of reference, stitch design.

Stitch, using four plies of floss and working the cross-stitches over two threads of fabric.

Steam-press the stitcheries on the wrong side. Trim stitcheries to 7x9 inches and baste to a piece of fleece. Refer to the general directions on pages 186–187 for completing pillows.

Bolster

Shown on pages 66–67.
Finished length is 17 inches, including end; circumference is 19 inches.
Design is 30 stitches high.

MATERIALS

17x25-inch piece of white hardanger
DMC No. 8 pearl cotton: 1 skein *each* of deep lavender (208), medium lavender (210), topaz (725), pale topaz (727), pumpkin (971), dark hunter green (3345), and light yellow-green (3348)
Polyester fiberfill, ¾ yard fabric
2 yards of 3½-inch-wide ungathered lace
1½ yards *each* of yellow and lavender ½-inch-wide satin ribbon
1¼ yards of ¹⁄₁₆-inch cord for piping

INSTRUCTIONS

Referring to pattern, *opposite,* chart design on graph paper. Note repeat of pattern. Baste 12x20-inch rectangle on fabric for bolster cover. Stitch repeat pattern along one long edge, leaving about 1½ inches between basting line and top of design.

Stitch, using one strand of pearl cotton and working the cross-stitches over two threads of fabric.

Trim embroidery to 12x20 inches. Cover cord for piping (see pages 186–187); stitch piping to long edges. *Note:* Use ½-inch seams throughout.

For ruffles, cut four 6x27-inch strips. Sew two strips end to end; repeat with remaining strips. Fold strips in half lengthwise; gather to 19 inches. Add gathered eyelet lace to each ruffle. Cut two 5x20-inch fabric pieces for bolster ends.

Pin right sides of bolster ends to ruffling. Pin all to long sides of embroidery. Sew through all layers along piping. Sew center back seam. Sew casings in ends for ribbons. Stuff; pull ribbons to gather ends and tie into bows.

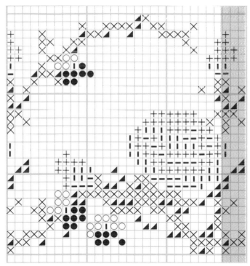

Bolster and Curtain Tiebacks

COLOR KEY
- ◉ Deep Lavender (208)
- ◯ Medium Lavender (210)
- ⊞ Topaz (725)
- ⊞ Pale Topaz (727)
- ⊟ Pumpkin (971)
- ⊠ Dark Hunter Green (3345)
- ◢ Light Yellow Green (3348)

Curtain Tiebacks

Shown on page 67.
Finished size is 4⅜ inches wide.
Design is 30 stitches high.

MATERIALS
For a pair of tiebacks
14x28-inch piece of white 18-count Aida cloth
DMC embroidery floss: 2 skeins of dark hunter green (3345) and 1 skein *each* of deep lavender (208), medium lavender (210), topaz (725), pale topaz (727), pumpkin (971), and light yellow-green (3348)
Polyester fleece, cord for piping
½-inch-diameter plastic rings
Fabric for backing and piping
Embroidery hoop
Tapestry needle

INSTRUCTIONS
Before beginning, see the general information on pages 180–183 for special cross-stitch tips and techniques, and for materials necessary for working all counted cross-stitch projects.

Referring to pattern, *opposite,* chart design onto graph paper. Cut fabric into two 7x28-inch pieces. Baste a line along horizontal center of fabric. Stitch five pattern repeats along line in the center of the strip. (The backs of the curtain tiebacks are not stitched.)

Use four plies of floss and work the cross-stitches over two threads of the fabric.

Mark strip to 4¼x23 inches. Cover cord for piping. Complete the same as for Prairie Rose Napkin Caddies (see page 34.)

Four-Seasons Throw

Shown on pages 68–69.

MATERIALS
One Gloria cloth panel (available from Joan Toggitt, Ltd.; see Instructions, below)
DMC embroidery floss: 3 skeins *each* of dark violet (552), dark dusty rose (961), hunter green (3346), and medium yellow-green (3347); 2 skeins *each of* avocado green (469), deep violet (550), light violet (554), light old gold (676), medium old gold (729), light olive green (734), copper (921), deep forest green (986), and medium forest green (988); and 1 skein *each* of light steel gray (318), dark hazelnut brown (420), tan (436), light avocado green (470), very pale avocado green (472), dark bittersweet (720), topaz (725), medium yellow (743), medium topaz (782), medium garnet (815), deep coral red (817), medium dusty rose (962), pale dusty rose (963), forest green (989), medium salmon (3328), and dark hunter green (3345)
Embroidery hoop, tapestry needle

INSTRUCTIONS
Before beginning, see the general information on pages 180–183 for special cross-stitch tips and techniques, and for materials necessary for working all counted cross-stitch projects.

Note: Gloria cloth is sold by the piece and features a rectangular band that is defined by rows of raised stitches. This design is stitched within the area defined by the raised stitches. A long side of stitching area contains 53x399 threads; a short side contains 53x285 threads; the corner squares contain 53x53 threads.

Stitch, using six plies of floss and working the cross-stitches over two threads.

Referring to patterns, *below,* to positioning diagram, *right,* and to photograph, page 69, stitch corner motifs in stitching area.

For the sides of the throw, use the charts on page 77. Flanking each corner motif is the corresponding strip of foliage for that season. Stitch the entire pattern on a long side; stitch a shortened version on a short side.

Refer to position diagram, *right,* and note letters that indicate placement of each of the long foliage patterns. Stitch the long version of the foliage patterns adjacent to the corner blocks, leaving four threads unworked. Then, omitting the shaded portion of the foliage pattern, stitch across the ends of the throw, again leaving four threads unworked.

BACKSTITCHES: In the corners, work the tulip stem using avocado green (469); work the pumpkin vines using dark hunter green (3345); work the sun's rays using topaz (725). On the rose motif, work the thorns using medium yellow-green (3347).

Steam-press on the wrong side.

To make fringe, machine-zigzag-stitch 7 inches beyond raised stitches defining stitching area. Pull threads.

Spring Corner	Spring Shortened	Winter Shortened	Winter Corner
Spring Complete			Winter Complete
Fall Complete			Summer Complete
Fall Corner	Fall Shortened	Summer Shortened	Summer Corner

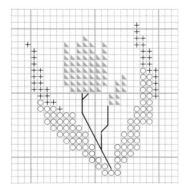 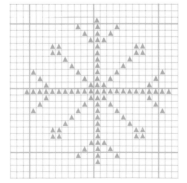 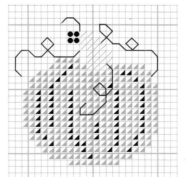 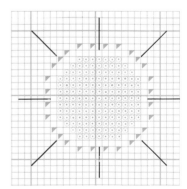

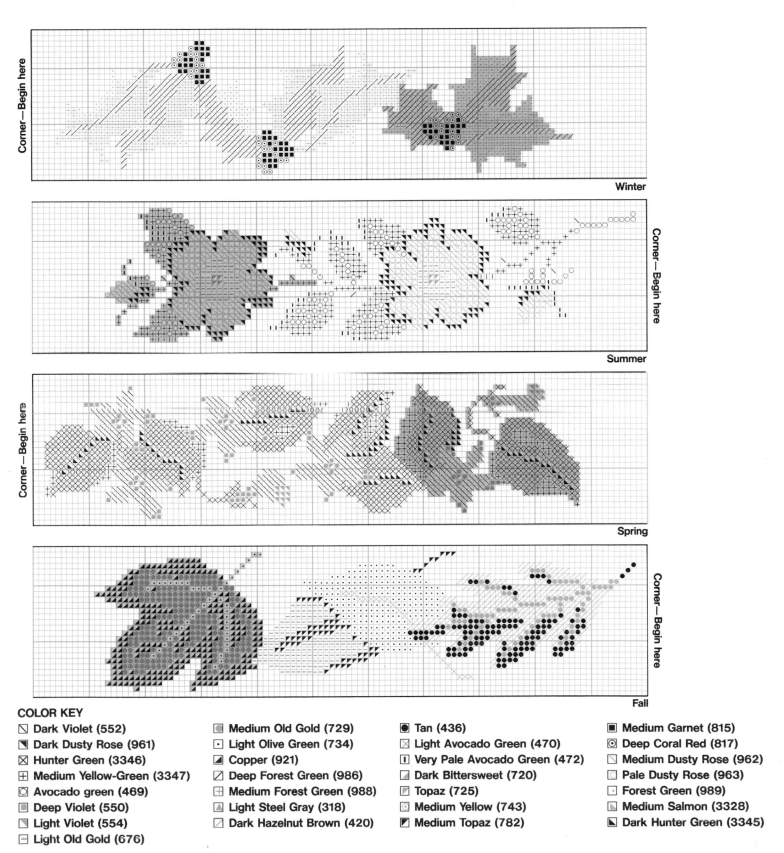

Corner—Begin here

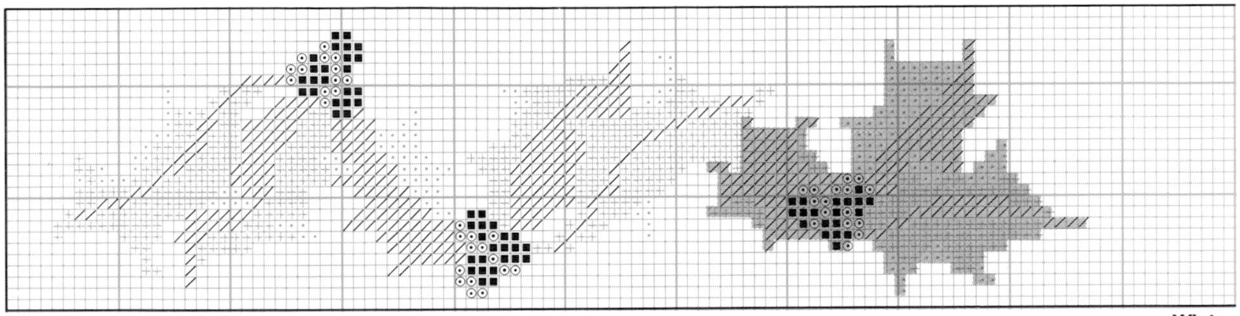

Winter

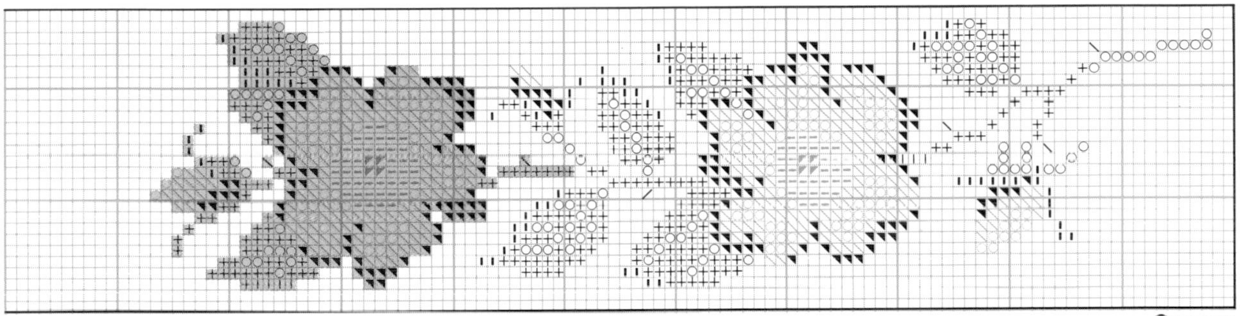

Corner—Begin here

Summer

Corner—Begin here

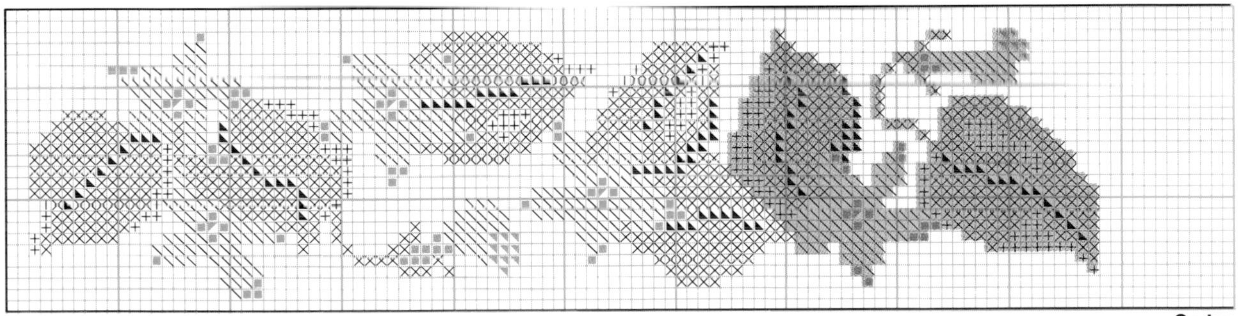

Spring

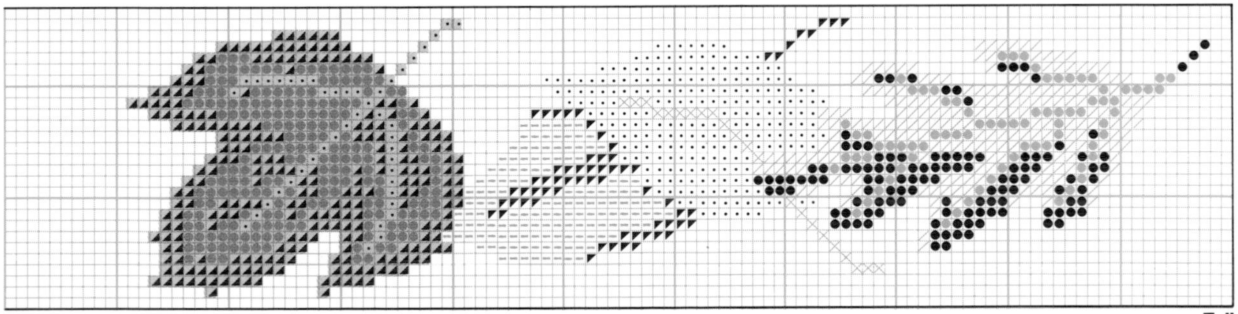

Corner—Begin here

Fall

COLOR KEY

- Dark Violet (552)
- Dark Dusty Rose (961)
- Hunter Green (3346)
- Medium Yellow-Green (3347)
- Avocado green (469)
- Deep Violet (550)
- Light Violet (554)
- Light Old Gold (676)
- Medium Old Gold (729)
- Light Olive Green (734)
- Copper (921)
- Deep Forest Green (986)
- Medium Forest Green (988)
- Light Steel Gray (318)
- Dark Hazelnut Brown (420)
- Tan (436)
- Light Avocado Green (470)
- Very Pale Avocado Green (472)
- Dark Bittersweet (720)
- Topaz (725)
- Medium Yellow (743)
- Medium Topaz (782)
- Medium Garnet (815)
- Deep Coral Red (817)
- Medium Dusty Rose (962)
- Pale Dusty Rose (963)
- Forest Green (989)
- Medium Salmon (3328)
- Dark Hunter Green (3345)

A Flag Alphabet In Nautical Code

Sailors and landlubbers alike will delight in these projects based on the international signal flag alphabet. These colorful flags—each bright shape represents either a letter of the alphabet or a numeral—are used to identify ships at sea and property. In this chapter, cross-stitch adaptations of the letters form monograms and initials.

Several motifs familiar to boaters make up the Nautical Sampler, *opposite*. A pair of cutters flank the central compass motif. The square flags represent the signal alphabet; the tapered pennants above represent the numerals 1 through 0.

Instructions begin on page 82.

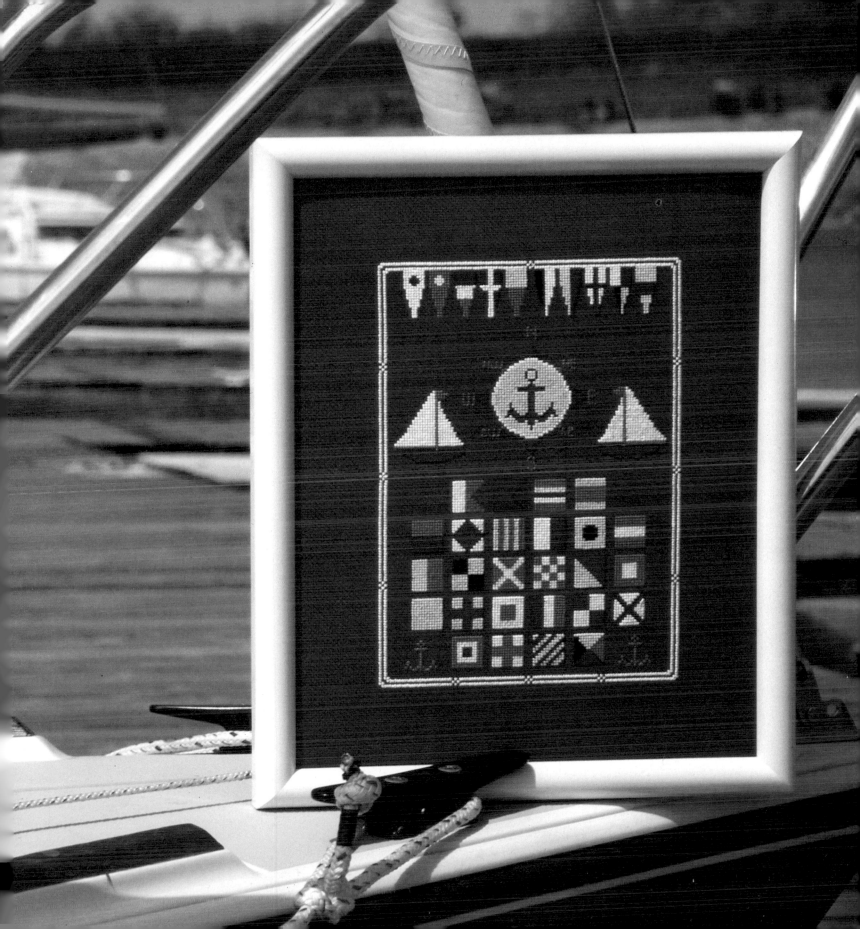

What better way to decorate a uniform than with a set of nautical initials. The first mate's sweatshirt, *opposite,* features his initials stitched onto the fabric. Using waste canvas simplifies stitching, and the finished shirt is just as machine-washable as a plain one.

The set of coasters, *above left,* is designed to show off embroidery. Here, each flag is stitched onto perforated paper. Then the stitcheries are cut into circles and inserted beneath the protective plastic covering.

Every swabbie needs a duffel to stow away gear, and the cross-stitched tag, *above right,* makes a quick-to-spot label. As with all of the nautical flag projects, it's made of any combination of "letters."

For travelers on land or sea, the case, *left,* is a handy cache for maps, directions, and other information. The focal point is the compass, but you might embellish the case further by stitching a family name in signal flags.

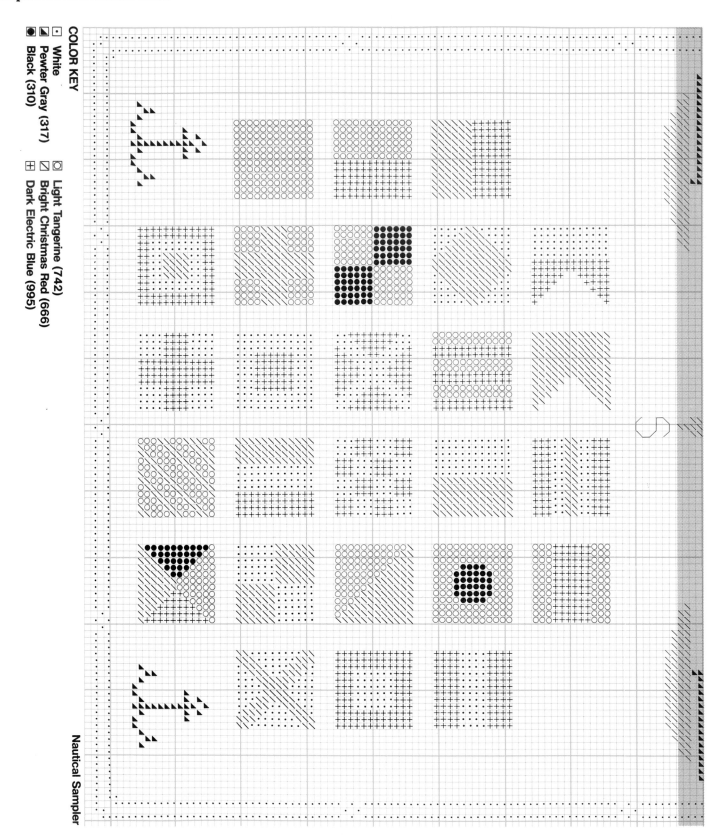

COLOR KEY

⊡	◣	⬤
White	Pewter Gray (317)	Black (310)

▣	◫	⊞
Light Tangerine (742)	Bright Christmas Red (666)	Dark Electric Blue (995)

82

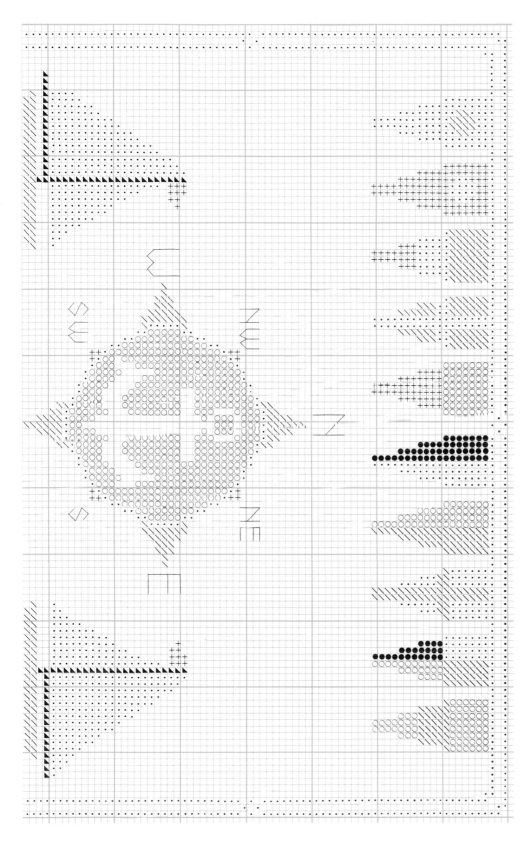

Nautical Sampler

Shown on page 79.
Finished size is 6¾x9¼ inches.
Design is 119x163 stitches.

MATERIALS

20x21-inch piece of navy 18-count
  Davosa fabric
DMC embroidery floss: 2 skeins of
  white and 1 skein *each* of black
  (310), pewter gray (317), bright
  Christmas red (666), light tangerine
  (742), and dark electric blue (995)
Embroidery hoop
Tapestry needle

INSTRUCTIONS

Before beginning, see the general information on pages 180–183 for special cross-stitch tips and techniques, and for materials necessary for working all counted cross-stitch projects.

Referring to pattern, *left,* chart sampler onto graph paper.

Measure 7 inches down from the top and 7 inches in from the left edge of the fabric. Begin stitching the upper-left corner of the border here.

Stitch, using two plies of floss and working the cross-stitches over one thread of fabric.

Work N, NE, E, SE, S, SW, W, and NW in backstitches using pewter gray (317).

Steam-press the stitchery on the wrong side.

Frame the sampler as desired.

Monogrammed Sweatshirt

Shown on page 80.
Finished size of each initial is 1¼x1¼ inches.

MATERIALS
Sweatshirt
10-count waste canvas sufficiently large for initials desired, plus 1 inch
DMC embroidery floss: Small amounts of each of the 5 colors used for flag alphabet; see materials list for Nautical Sampler, page 83
Embroidery hoop, tapestry needle

INSTRUCTIONS
Before beginning, see the general information on pages 180–183 for special cross-stitch tips and techniques, and for materials necessary for working all counted cross-stitch projects.

Referring to pattern for Nautical Sampler, pages 82–83, chart initials desired for monogram.

The alphabet appears in five rows at the bottom of the sampler. Letters A, B, C, and D are in the first row; letters E, F, G, H, I, and J are in the second row; letters K, L, M, N, O, and P are in the third row; letters Q, R, S, T, U, and V are in the fourth row; and letters W, X, Y, and Z are in the fifth row.

Baste waste canvas onto the front of the sweatshirt, either centered or slightly toward the left-hand side. Stitch design, using three plies of floss and working cross-stitches over one thread of waste canvas.

After the design is stitched, trim waste canvas ¼ inch past stitching. Dampen stitchery with warm water; gently pull threads of canvas from beneath cross-stitches.

When dry, press with a warm iron.

Nautical Coasters

Shown on page 81.
Finished size of each initial is approximately 1¾x1¾ inches.

MATERIALS
Set of coasters designed to receive needlework inserts
Scraps of white perforated paper
DMC embroidery floss: Small amounts of each of the 5 colors used for flag alphabet; see materials list for Nautical Sampler, page 83
Tapestry needle

INSTRUCTIONS
Before beginning, see the general information on pages 180–183 for special cross-stitch tips and techniques, and for materials necessary for working all counted cross-stitch projects.

Referring to pattern for Nautical Sampler, pages 82–83, chart initials desired for coasters.

The alphabet appears in five rows at the bottom of the sampler. Letters A, B, C, and D are in the first row; letters E, F, G, H, I, and J are in the second row; letters K, L, M, N, O, and P are in the third row; letters Q, R, S, T, U, and V are in the fourth row; and letters W, X, Y, and Z are in the fifth row.

Stitch a single initial onto a scrap of perforated paper. Use four plies of floss and work the cross-stitches over two squares of perforated paper.

Following manufacturer's directions, insert paper into coasters.

Luggage Tag

Shown on page 81.
Finished size is 6¾x2⅜ inches.

MATERIALS
Scrap of red 18-count Davosa fabric

DMC embroidery floss: Small amounts of each of the 5 colors used for flag alphabet; see materials list for Nautical Sampler, page 83
Scrap of polyester fleece
Scrap of backing fabric
¾ yard of narrow piping, metal eyelet
Scrap of clear vinyl
Medium-weight paper
Water-erasable marking pen

INSTRUCTIONS
Before beginning, see the general information on pages 180–183 for special cross-stitch tips and techniques, and for materials necessary for working all counted cross-stitch projects.

Referring to pattern for Nautical Sampler, pages 82–83, chart initials desired for luggage tag.

The alphabet appears in five rows at the bottom of the sampler. Letters A, B, C, and D are in the first row; letters E, F, G, H, I, and J are in the second row; letters K, L, M, N, O, and P are in the third row; letters Q, R, S, T, U, and V are in the fourth row; and letters W, X, Y, and Z are in the fifth row.

Stitch, using four plies of floss and working the cross-stitches over two threads of fabric. Leave six threads of fabric unworked between each motif.

Steam-press on the wrong side.

With marking pen, draw rectangle on fabric ½ inch past completed stitchery, tapering left-hand end to a point (see photograph, page 81). Sew fleece to back of stitchery along line. Sew piping to this stitching line. With right sides facing, sew backing fabric to stitchery along piping line, leaving several inches open for turning. Trim seam to ¼ inch; clip corners and turn. Press. Slip-stitch closed.

Cut paper and vinyl to fit backing. Print or type label for tag as desired. Layer paper on backing; top with vinyl piece. Topstitch through all layers close to piping.

Install eyelet near point of tag.

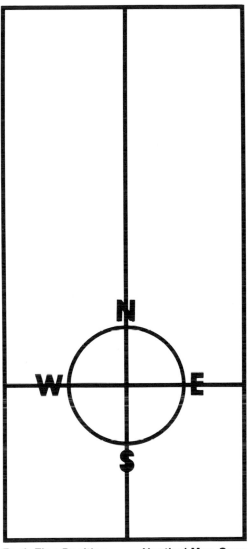

Back Flap Position   **Nautical Map Case**

Map Case

Shown on page 81.
Finished size is 7¼x11½ inches.

MATERIALS

11x24-inch piece of navy 18-count Davosa fabric (back of case and flap)
9x13-inch piece of navy 18-count Davosa fabric (front of case)
DMC embroidery floss: 1 skein *each* of white, bright Christmas red (666), light tangerine (742), and dark electric blue (995)
½ yard fabric for lining
2 yards narrow piping to match lining
½ yard fleece, large snap
Water-erasable marking pen

INSTRUCTIONS

Before beginning, see the general information on pages 180–183 for special cross-stitch tips and techniques, and for materials necessary for working all counted cross-stitch projects.

This case is made from two pieces of even-weave fabric: a long strip that forms the back and top flap and a shorter strip for the front.

Referring to pattern, pages 82–83, and position diagram, *left,* chart center compass design on graph paper. Lay out longer strip of fabric on a work surface. Baste a line along lengthwise (24-inch) center. Then baste a perpendicular line (11 inches long) 7 inches from one short end. Where these lines intersect is the center of the compass motif. Position design so that the top (north) is along lengthwise center and approximately 10 inches from one short end. (*Note:* Remember that this piece folds over to form the case flap.) See position diagram, *left.*

Stitch, using four plies of floss and working the cross-stitches over two threads of fabric.

Work N, NE, E, SE, S, SW, W, and NW in dark electric blue (995). Steam-press the stitchery on the wrong side.

With marking pen, draw a 7¼-inch square around compass motif for flap outline; draw two diagonal lines along SW and SE sides to make pointed flap. Then draw a 7¼x11½-inch rectangle adjacent to motif for back of case. For case front, draw a 7¼x11-inch rectangle on shorter strip of Davosa fabric.

Cut out both pieces, adding ½-inch seam allowances. Cut out matching shapes from fleece.

Layer fabric and fleece pieces; stitch together along marking lines. Sew piping to back/flap piece along same line. Sew piping to top edge of front piece; trim fleece seam allowance and press seam to wrong side.

With right sides facing and aligning bottom edges, sew front to back on piping line, leaving top open. Trim allowances to ¼ inch and clip corners.

Cut lining fabric to 8¼x20 inches. Fold together right sides of lining piece to match shape of case; stitch side seams. With right sides facing, sew lining flap to case flap along piping line; trim seam allowances to ¼ inch. Clip corners. Turn flap right side out; press. Tuck lining into case. Slip-stitch lining to piping line along top edge of case front. Sew on snap for closure.

If desired, spell out family name or initials with nautical code alphabet; position "letters" near bottom of front or on back of map case. To create initials with flag alphabet, see instructions for Luggage Tag, page 84.

Delightful Designs For Nursery And Playroom

Because of the broad appeal of cross-stitch, creating magical designs for children is as easy as achieving sophisticated and elegant looks. This chapter includes projects and designs that are right at home in any kid's room.

One effective use of the quartet of animal patterns featured in this chapter is to make a crib mobile, *right*. Each design is worked twice—the second one is a mirror image of the first so that each figure has a stitched front and back. Then they're sewn together, stuffed, and suspended on ribbons from wooden dowels.

Each of the four is scaled for use as part of a group, though the designs also can be used singly, as they are on the bibs, *above*.

Instructions begin on page 92.

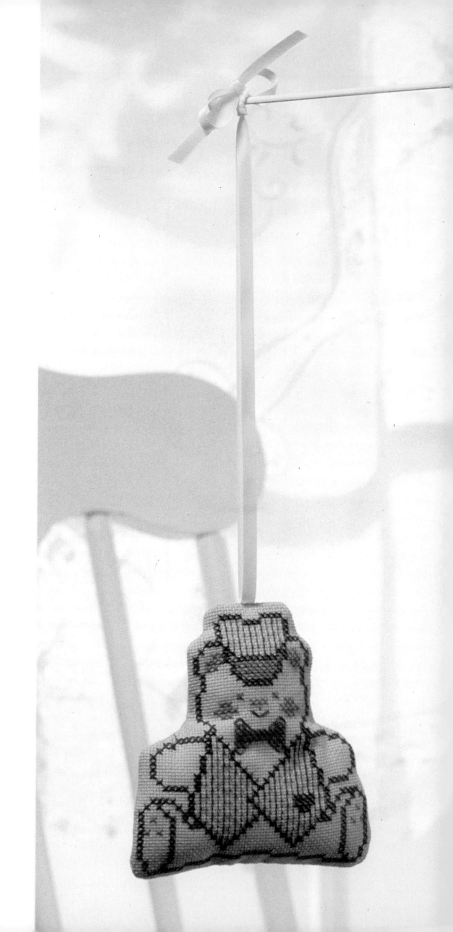

For that tangle of cold-weather gear that accumulates around doorways, the mitten holder, *opposite,* is a convenient solution.

Four cross-stitched mittens, each with a distinctive pattern and personality, are lined up across the plaque. To complete the mitten holder, pad it with quilt batting and wrap it around a piece of plywood or lumber, or around a set of stretcher strips. Add as many decorative hooks as you need.

The tiny framed stitcheries *above* are reminiscent of Victorian cameos. Each country-style silhouette fits inside an oval border, and the overall shape is adaptable to round, oval, or square frames.

Once the boy and girl motifs are stitched in any color desired, put them to a variety of uses. Add a baby's name and birth date beneath the ovals to make a miniature birth announcement. Or work the designs without any greeting on fabric with a larger stitch count to make a pocket for a toddler's jumper or overalls.

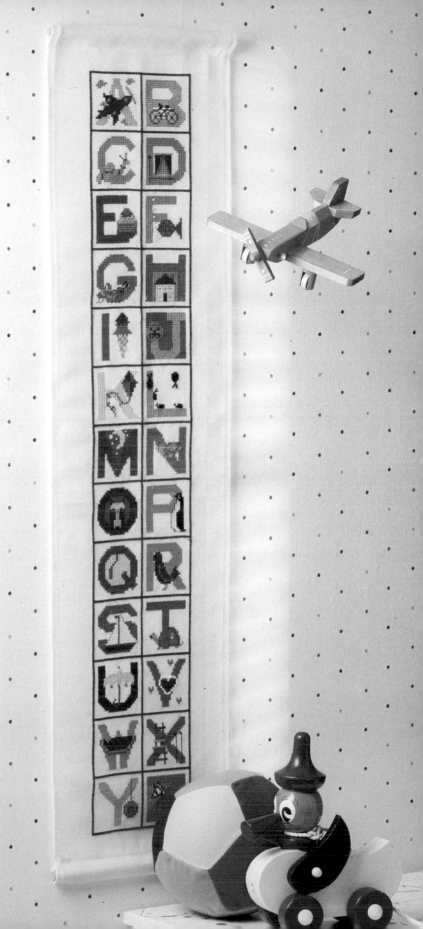

Devising clever alphabets for kids is one assignment that most children's illustrators relish. This assortment of cross-stitched letters and their accompanying objects is a fine tool for budding abecedarians.

To showcase each of these intriguing letters, a colorful banner like the one *right* is most effective. Simply stitch 13 pairs of boxes and fill in each square with a letter. Add dowels in casings at the top and bottom so that the banner hangs crisply.

For a more personal stitchery, use the letters to create individual names or initials. Because the canvas seat back is so easy to apply stitchery to, the director's chair, *opposite,* is a winning candidate for such identification.

Another easy way to use this alphabet is to stitch one, two, or three initials on a sweatshirt or denim jacket. Baste a square of waste canvas to the garment where the initial looks best. Work the cross-stitches over the waste canvas. When the stitching is completed, dampen the canvas with water and pull away the canvas threads (leaving the stitching intact).

Crib Mobile

Shown on pages 86–87.

MATERIALS
8x16-inch pieces of pink, light blue, light yellow, and tan 14-count Aida cloth
Susan Bates Anchor embroidery floss: 1 skein *each* of peach (10), red (19), pink (25), rose (28), violet (98), light blue (146), blue (148), green (210), yellow (297), light orange (313), orange (316), brown (341), gray (398), and black (403)
Polyester fiberfill
⅛-inch-diameter dowels
Painted wooden beads
Enamel paint
¼-inch-wide satin ribbon
Embroidery hoop
Tapestry needle

INSTRUCTIONS
Before beginning, see the general information on pages 180–183 for special cross-stitch tips and techniques, and for materials necessary for working all counted cross-stitch projects.

Referring to patterns for cat, duck, bear, and dog, *opposite,* transfer designs to graph paper with felt-tip markers. Then chart a mirror-image design on graph paper for the back of each figure. Note horizontal and vertical centers of each of the patterns.

Cut fabrics into 8x8-inch squares. Baste horizontal and vertical centers of each piece of fabric.

Use two plies of floss, and work the cross-stitches over one thread of the fabric.

Using basted lines and center lines of chart as reference points, stitch designs. For mobile shown, you will need a front and back of each figure—the back is a mirror image of the front.

BACKSTITCHES: For cat, work mouth, eyebrows, and whiskers in vi-

olet (98). Work running stitches on body, feet, and tail in rose (28).

For duck, work eyes and outline bill, tie, and feet in blue (148).

For dog, work eyebrows and one stitch above bell in black (403). Add a French knot clapper beneath bell in red (19).

For bear, work vertical stitch at lip in orange (316); work mouth in red (19). Work vertical stripes on vest and cap in red (19) and light blue (146), alternating colors every row and aligning cap stripes with vest stripes. Backstitch tie in red (19).

Steam-press on wrong side.

Place with right sides facing. Refer to general directions, pages 186–187, for completing an ornament.

ASSEMBLY: Cut dowels to 17 and 8 inches. Paint; when dry, attach wooden beads onto ends of dowels. Suspend a figure from both ends of each dowel with ribbon; trim with small bows. Suspend the smaller dowel from a length of ribbon so that dowel is balanced. Then attach this ribbon to the longer dowel. Attach a length of ribbon to longer dowel for hanging. Adjust balance of mobile by sliding ribbons. Secure all ribbons with glue.

Keepsake Bibs

Shown on page 86.
Finished diameter is 9½ inches.

MATERIALS
For each bib
12x12-inch piece of white 18-count even-weave fabric
Susan Bates Anchor embroidery floss: See instructions, *left,* and charts, *opposite,* for Crib Mobile for colors used for each figure
Polyester fleece
Fabric for backing, binding, and ties
Scraps of narrow rickrack

INSTRUCTIONS
Before beginning, see the general information on pages 180–183 for special cross-stitch tips and techniques, and for materials necessary for working all counted cross-stitch projects.

Referring to instructions and charts for Crib Mobile, stitch one figure in center of fabric for each bib. Use three plies of floss and work the cross-stitches over two threads of fabric.

Steam-press the stitchery on the wrong side.

ASSEMBLY: Draw a 9½-inch-diameter circle on tissue paper. At top of circle, draw a 3½-inch-diameter half-circle for neck cutout. Cut out bib pattern. Centering stitched design, cut out bib; cut out fleece and backing fabric to match.

Layer stitchery and fleece; baste together. Stitch rickrack 1 inch inside cut edge of pattern, positioning ends of rickrack at bottom of bib. Conceal ends with rickrack bow.

Layer stitchery and fleece atop backing. Bind edges with strips of bias-cut fabric. Center and stitch a 28-inch piece of bias to neck edge, sewing to ends of tie extensions.

Name Plaque

Shown on page 89.
Finished size of stitchery is approximately 2x3 inches.
Design is 38 stitches wide and 53 stitches high.

MATERIALS
6x7-inch piece of white 18-count Aida cloth
Embroidery floss: 1 skein *each* of 2 colors (for best results use 2 shades of the same color, such as medium blue and light blue)
Small purchased frame
Embroidery hoop, tapestry needle

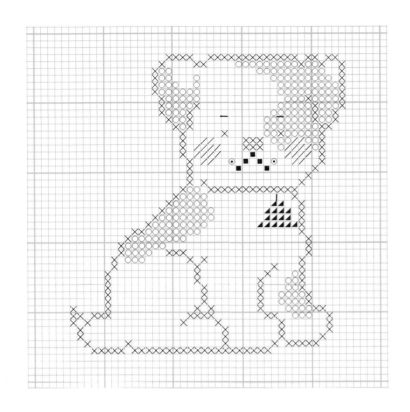

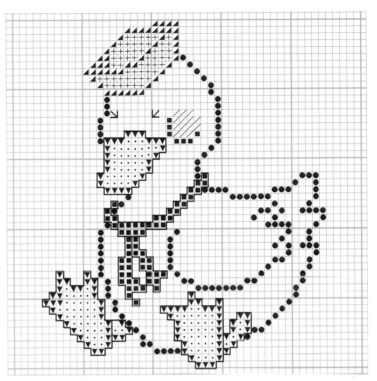

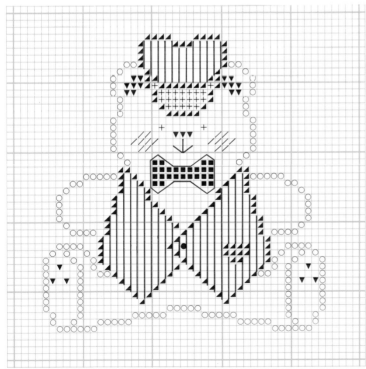

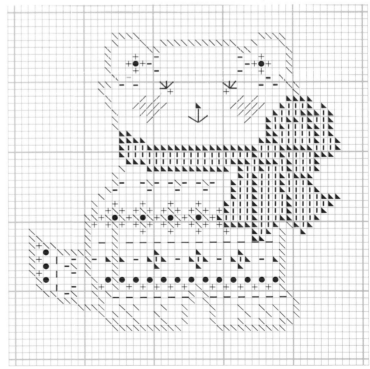

Crib Mobiles and Baby Bibs

COLOR KEY

⬈ Peach (10)	◧ Rose (28)	◩ Blue (148)
◼ Red (19)	◺ Violet (98)	⊟ Green (210)
⊡ Pink (25)	⊞ Light Blue (146)	⬤ Yellow (297)

⊡ Light Orange (313)	◉ Gray (398)
▼ Orange (316)	⊠ Black (403)
◎ Brown (341)	

93

Boy Profile Plaque

Girl Profile Plaque

INSTRUCTIONS

Before beginning, see the general information on pages 180–183 for special cross-stitch tips and techniques, and for materials necessary for working all counted cross-stitch projects.

Referring to pattern for boy and girl designs, *left,* chart either design on graph paper. Use main color as indicated by the Xs on the pattern; use contrasting color for circles on the pattern. Mark horizontal and vertical centers. Baste centers of fabric.

Use two plies of floss and work the cross-stitches over one thread of the fabric.

Stitch design on fabric, using center lines as points of reference. Add child's name or other greeting beneath motif, using any of the small alphabets in this book.

Steam-press the stitchery on the wrong side, and frame.

Mitten Holder

Shown on page 88.
Finished size is 9x15 inches.
Design is 155 stitches wide and 74 stitches high.

MATERIALS

14x20-inch piece of white 11-count
  Aida cloth
DMC embroidery floss: 1 skein *each*
  of bright Christmas red (666), light
  Christmas green (701), light
  tangerine (742), royal blue (797),
  and dark navy blue (823)
14x20-inch piece of white backing
  fabric
14x16-inch piece of quilt batting
3 decorative hooks
9-inch and 15-inch stretcher strips (or
  a 9x15-inch piece of lumber or ¾-
  inch plywood)
Staple gun
Embroidery hoop
Tapestry needle

INSTRUCTIONS

Before beginning, see the general information on pages 180–183 for special cross-stitch tips and techniques, and for materials necessary for working all counted cross-stitch projects.

Chart pattern, *opposite,* onto graph paper. Mark horizontal and vertical centers of chart; baste horizontal and vertical centers of fabric. Stitch design, using center lines as reference points.

Use three plies of floss and work the cross-stitches over one thread of fabric.

Steam-press the stitchery on the wrong side. Layer backing, batting, and stitchery; baste around the perimeter of the assembly.

Assemble stretcher strips or sand edges of plywood. Center stitchery atop assembled strips or backing, leaving sufficient room at bottom for hooks. Smooth and stretch stitchery to back, and staple in place. Mark stitchery for hooks, spacing each one equally, and attach hooks to backing material.

ABC Banner

Shown on page 91.
Finished size is 9x35 inches.
Design is 55 stitches wide and 352 stitches high.

MATERIALS

12x44-inch piece of white hardanger
DMC embroidery floss: 3 skeins of
  bright Christmas red (666); 2
  skeins *each* of plum (718) and
  deep emerald green (909); and 1
  skein *each* of white, black (310),
  pewter gray (317), dark mahogany
  (400), light hazelnut brown (422),
  dark violet (552), cranberry (603),
  medium yellow (743), deep
  cornflower blue (791), royal blue
  (797), medium delft (799), medium

garnet (815), light parrot green (907), pumpkin (971), and deep canary (972)
Wooden dowel
Embroidery hoop
Tapestry needle

INSTRUCTIONS

Before beginning, see the general information on pages 180–183 for special cross-stitch tips and techniques, and for materials necessary for working all counted cross-stitch projects.

Chart alphabet patterns, pages 96–97, onto graph paper.

Measure 3½ inches down from the top and 3½ inches in from left side; begin stitching upper-left corner of border here. Mount fabric in hoop and start cross-stitching with outside border. Stitch, using three plies of floss and working the cross-stitches over two threads of fabric.

For border, use bright Christmas red (666) and work across 55 stitches for top edge. Work down left and right long edges for a total of 352 stitches. Work a vertical center line down from top edge for 352 stitches. Work 55 stitches across bottom edge to enclose rectangle. Then work 12 more horizontal lines, spaced 26 stitches apart, to create boxes for letters. Red border, when stitched correctly, should have 13 rows of two squares each. The interior of each of the squares should have 26x26 stitches unworked for alphabet.

Stitch a letter inside each square, working A and B in top two squares, C and D in second row, E and F in third row, and so forth.

Trim, turn under, and press long edges so that finished width of chart is 9 inches. Fold under top and bottom edges 2 inches, leaving 1-inch-deep casings; stitch. Insert a 9-inch dowel in each casing.

Personalized Director's Chair

Shown on page 90.
Finished height of letters is 2½ inches.

MATERIALS

Director's chair
6-inch-wide strip of Davosa fabric as long as width of director's chair back plus 2 inches
DMC embroidery floss: See charts, pages 96–97, for colors of letters
Scraps of jumbo rickrack
Embroidery hoop
Tapestry needle

Mitten Holder

COLOR KEY

☑ Bright Christmas Red (666)	⊡ Light Tangerine (742)	⊠ Dark Navy Blue (823)
⊙ Light Christmas Green (701)	◉ Royal Blue (797)	

Delightful Designs for Nursery and Playroom

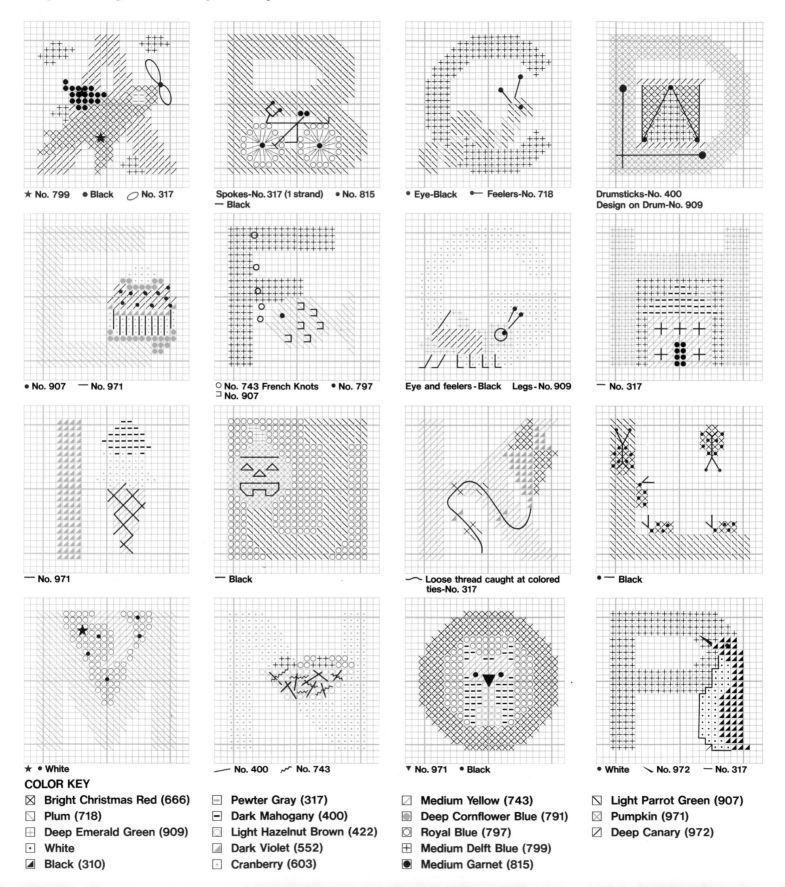

★ No. 799   ● Black   ◯ No. 317

Spokes-No. 317 (1 strand)   ● No. 815
— Black

● Eye-Black   •— Feelers-No. 718

Drumsticks-No. 400
Design on Drum-No. 909

● No. 907   — No. 971

○ No. 743 French Knots   ● No. 797
⊐ No. 907

Eye and feelers - Black   Legs-No. 909

— No. 317

— No. 971

— Black

⌒ Loose thread caught at colored
ties-No. 317

•— Black

★ ● White

— No. 400   ⌁ No. 743

▼ No. 971   ● Black

● White   ╲ No. 972   — No. 317

COLOR KEY

⊠ **Bright Christmas Red (666)**

◹ **Plum (718)**

⊞ **Deep Emerald Green (909)**

⊡ **White**

◪ **Black (310)**

⊟ **Pewter Gray (317)**

⊟ **Dark Mahogany (400)**

◰ **Light Hazelnut Brown (422)**

◩ **Dark Violet (552)**

⬚ **Cranberry (603)**

◹ **Medium Yellow (743)**

◉ **Deep Cornflower Blue (791)**

◎ **Royal Blue (797)**

⊞ **Medium Delft Blue (799)**

◉ **Medium Garnet (815)**

◺ **Light Parrot Green (907)**

⊠ **Pumpkin (971)**

◹ **Deep Canary (972)**

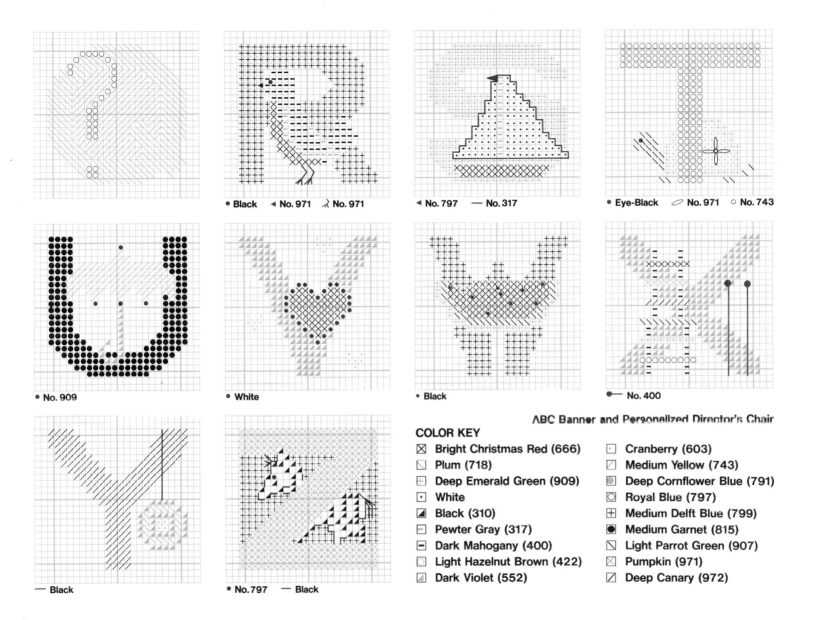

• Black **◄ No. 971** **⅄ No. 971**   **◄ No. 797** **— No. 317**   **• Eye-Black** **⟋ No. 971** **○ No. 743**

• No. 909   **• White**   **• Black**   **●— No. 400**

ABC Banner and Personalized Director's Chair

— Black   **• No. 797** **— Black**

COLOR KEY

⊠	Bright Christmas Red (666)	⊡	Cranberry (603)
◩	Plum (718)	▱	Medium Yellow (743)
⊞	Deep Emerald Green (909)	▣	Deep Cornflower Blue (791)
⊡	White	⊙	Royal Blue (797)
◪	Black (310)	⊞	Medium Delft Blue (799)
⊟	Pewter Gray (317)	●	Medium Garnet (815)
⊟	Dark Mahogany (400)	◩	Light Parrot Green (907)
▢	Light Hazelnut Brown (422)	⊠	Pumpkin (971)
◪	Dark Violet (552)	◱	Deep Canary (972)

INSTRUCTIONS

Before beginning, see the general information on pages 180–183 for special cross-stitch tips and techniques, and for materials necessary for working all counted cross-stitch projects.

Referring to alphabet patterns, *opposite* and *above,* chart letters for name onto graph paper, leaving four stitches between letters. Mark horizontal and vertical centers of chart. Baste horizontal and vertical centers of fabric.

Stitch, using four plies of floss and working the cross-stitches over two threads of fabric. Use centers as marked for points of reference.

Steam-press the stitchery on the wrong side.

Using a water-erasable pen, draw a horizontal line 1 inch above and 1 inch below stitching; trim fabric ½ inch past line. Fold under short edges of stitchery to align with side edges of chairback.

Rip casing seams along short ends of chairback.

Center and stitch rickrack along marked lines; fold under raw edges of fabric and half of rickrack to wrong side to form rickrack points. Press. Center stitchery on chairback; topstitch just below rickrack points and along short ends. Fold casings back in place; machine-stitch to secure.

A Treasury
Of
Antique Samplers

Most early examples of cross-stitch embroidery that remain for us to enjoy are samplers. The samplers were made from materials that have endured for generations, and have been passed from parent to child as family heirlooms. This chapter contains three samplers based on antique stitcheries.

The sampler design, *opposite,* is filled with elegant alphabets and charmingly stylized flowers and animals. The central tree-of-life motif, a common element in many samplers of the 18th and 19th centuries, uses lazy daisy stitches for its foliage.

Instructions and charts for the three samplers in this chapter begin on page 104. Photographs of the original renditions of these designs appear on pages 102 and 103.

Mixing motifs of varying—and often illogical—proportions is what gives early samplers their charm and appeal. The sampler, *opposite,* for example, features birds, blossoms, and fruit in disproportionate sizes.

The original version of this sampler (see pages 102 and 103) was stitched with variegated yarn. The updated version shown here uses five subtle shades of pink Persian yarn to duplicate the effect.

Parts of the sampler, *right,* are stitched over one thread, and the remainder is stitched over two threads. Although no one knows whether the stitcher's intention was to display her skill at fine craftsmanship or merely to fill odd spaces, the sampler remains a beautiful combination of alphabets and an intriguing representation of the stitcher's world.

Cross-Stitch Antiques

Here's a look at how the craft of cross-stitch developed.

When today's stitchers begin work on a cross-stitch sampler, they are continuing a centuries-old tradition of embroidery. Cross-stitch—and especially all of the various forms of samplers—is the outgrowth of a rich and diverse background, with influences from all around the world.

The word "sampler" is from the Latin *exemplar,* meaning "pattern," and that's exactly what the early samplers were. In the 16th and 17th centuries, samplers were stitched on long, narrow pieces of linen, and were records of random stitches in the days before embroiderers had pattern books to follow. The expense and scarcity of paper made it difficult to record designs, so the sampler strips became valuable teaching devices and reference sources. As a young girl learned a new stitch, she added it to the strip in random patterns. These early samplers could be rolled up and tucked away until embroiderers needed to refer to a certain stitch or technique.

A classroom activity

During the 18th century, however, sampler stitchery moved out of the home and into the school, where it became part of the curriculum for thousands of young girls. Along with geography and reading, the girls learned the art of "ornamental" needlework, which included sampler stitchery. Far from the basic sewing every girl learned at home, the ornamentals were imaginative, and a true test of stitchery skill. Because of this, a girl won respect based on the exper-

tise she showed in her stitches.

Making samplers gave girls the opportunity to practice embroidery while they learned to read, write, and memorize virtues. In the late 1700s, when only four of 10 women could write their names, stitching an alphabet, signatures, and a moral verse was quite an accomplishment. Sampler stitching was not always popular with these schoolgirls, however. One girl stated on hers that she hated every stitch; she liked to read much more.

Perhaps because of this required ac-

tivity, samplers took on a new look; 18th-century samplers became more diversified in design. Samplers of this period included biblical or sentimental verses, human figures, and pictorial scenes.

Needle-art academies

Apparently, the first American academy to teach needlework opened in Boston in 1706. Others soon followed, and advertisements such as this one from a 1784 *Boston Gazette* were common in northeastern newspapers: "Misses Sutherlands . . . have opened a Boarding & Day School, for young Ladies . . . where they will be carefully instructed in all kinds of Fine Needle Work, Embroidery . . . ."

By the end of the Revolutionary War, needle-art academies were springing up all over the Northeast. Several of the academies were led by women who had developed distinc-

tive styles of sampler design.

In the 1700s, for instance, Sarah Stivour's school in Salem developed a unique style using unraveled silk floss for cross-stitches and diagonal long stitches. These characteristics of a Stivour sampler have helped researchers trace stitcheries.

Mary Balch's academy

Mary Balch's Rhode Island academy, one of the most prominent eastern schools from 1785 to 1831, produced many sampler legacies. In fact, more existing samplers can be traced to this school than to any other. Balch developed several distinctive styles, including samplers that depicted local buildings. Along with reading, spelling, grammar, and good manners, her students learned to stitch replicas of churches and statehouses. In at least one instance, a Balch sampler has

provided important historical clues to the architecture of the time.

Samplers through time

Over the years, trends developed in sampler design. In fact, researchers often date samplers by the stitches and design elements used. In the 1700s, for example, borders became more prominent and embroiderers stitched more pictorial scenes. They also worked with novelty materials, such as sequins and beads. In the 1800s, the cross-stitch was used more heavily; designs were more open and even more pictorial than before.

Those stitchery pictures often included cartoonlike figures and charming scenes. Through them, girls portrayed such scenes as a New England meetinghouse complete with a giant butterfly overhead, or the figures of Adam and Eve in the Garden of Eden, with the serpent wrapped around the apple tree. Enormous birds, angels, vining flowers, and pristine New England villages also were popular subjects.

The alphabet always has been com-

mon to samplers, with two or three different forms often used on each sampler. An alphabet generally contained only 24 letters—the uppercase I and J were the same letter, as were the U and V.

Although girls changed their sampler designs and techniques, they used basically the same materials throughout the 18th and 19th centuries. Schoolgirls threaded their needles with silk floss and usually used linen for their sampler backgrounds. Some linen was imported, but the bulk of it was homemade. Occasionally, girls used wool fabric, and some examples still exist of samplers stitched on backgrounds of linsey-woolsey, named for its combination of linen and wool threads.

Once completed, samplers were considered family heirlooms, suitable not just for framing, but also for handing down from generation to generation. The samplers that included signatures were valued for their personal, positive proof of an ancestor's skill. In more recent times, researchers, too, have appreciated the identifications on the samplers.

Now, more than a century after needlework was dropped from the school curriculum, the appeal of samplers remains strong. Although the girls whose handiwork now hangs in the museums may never have foreseen the fate of their stitcheries, their painstaking work has created a visual record of history through several centuries of cross-stitch samplers.

Christian's Sampler

Shown on pages 98.
Finished size of sampler is 23½x18⅛ inches.
Design is 123 stitches wide and 163 stitches high.

MATERIALS

32x26-inch piece of white 18-count Aida cloth
DMC embroidery floss: 4 skeins of deep coral red (817); 2 skeins *each* of dark Christmas red (498), avocado green (469), and pale avocado green (471); and 1 skein *each* of dark antique violet (327), deep blue-green (500), topaz (725), medium cornflower blue (793), dark royal blue (796), and black-brown (3371)
Embroidery hoop
Tapestry needle

INSTRUCTIONS

Before beginning, see the general information on pages 180–183 for special cross-stitch tips and techniques, and for materials necessary for working all counted cross-stitch projects.

Referring to the pattern, *left*, chart design onto graph paper. Change initials to those of family members, or include a special date.

Stitch using three plies of floss and work the cross-stitches over two threads of fabric.

Measure 4 inches down from the top and 4 inches in from left side; begin stitching upper-left corner of border here. Fill in alphabets and motifs.

Work backstitches on the tree branches in deep blue-green (500), using three plies of floss. Work the lazy daisy stitches as indicated in pale avocado green (471) and avocado green (469) using six plies of floss.

Frame the sampler as desired.

COLOR KEY

⊠ Deep Coral Red (817)
⊞ Dark Christmas Red (498)
⊡ Avocado Green (469)
◎ Pale Avocado Green (471)
⊘ Dark Antique Violet (327)
● Deep Blue-Green (500)
⊡ Topaz (725)
▲ Medium Cornflower Blue (793)
◩ Dark Royal Blue (796)
■ Black-Brown (3371)

Lazy-daisy stitches:
⬫ Pale Avocado Green (471)
◯ Avocado Green (469)

Christian's Sampler

105

Mary's Sampler

COLOR KEY
- ⋅ Ice Blue (514)
- ⊠ Gray-Green (604)
- ◯ Yellow (753)
- ⊘ Light Pink (954)
- ◢ Green (662)
- ▼ Medium Pink (943)
- ⊞ Pale Pink (955)
- ◉ Deep Pink (940)
- ⊡ Dark Pink (941)
- ▣ Blue (501)

Mary's Sampler

Shown on page 100.
Finished size of stitchery is
15x19⅝ inches.
Design is 127 stitches wide and
171 stitches high.

MATERIALS

23x28-inch piece of cream 18-count
Congress cloth
Paternayan 3-ply Persian yarn (32-
inch lengths): 35 strands *each* of
ice blue (514) and gray-green (604);
30 strands *each* of yellow (753)
and light pink (954); 15 strands
each of green (662) and medium
pink (943); 10 strands of pale pink
(955); 7 strands *each* of deep pink
(940) and dark pink (941); and 5
strands of blue (501)
Additional Persian yarn as necessary
in colors desired for family names
and dates
Embroidery hoop
Tapestry needle

INSTRUCTIONS

Before beginning, see the general information on pages 180–183 for special cross-stitch tips and techniques,
and for materials necessary for working all counted cross-stitch projects.

Referring to the pattern, *left*, chart
design onto graph paper using felt-tip
markers. Add family name(s), initials
of family members, and a date after
the letter Z of the last alphabet. Or
chart a short verse, using one of the alphabets from this sampler.

Stitch, using two plies of Persian
yarn and working the cross-stitches
over two threads of fabric.

Measure 4 inches down from the
top and 4 inches over from left side;
begin stitching upper-left corner of
border here. Mount fabric in hoop and
start cross-stitching with outside border. Fill in alphabets and motifs.

Frame the sampler as desired.

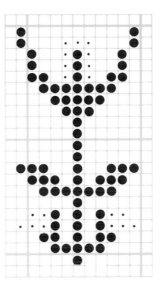

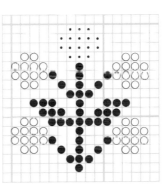

Margret's Sampler

Shown on page 101.
Finished size is 15⅝x20½ inches.
Design is 141x185 stitches.

MATERIALS
24x28-inch piece of 18-count beige
  Davosa fabric
DMC embroidery floss: 4 skeins of
  dark salmon (347); 3 skeins *each*
  of dark blue-green (501) and light
  terra-cotta (758); 2 skeins *each* of
  dark hazelnut brown (420) and
  medium blue-green (503); and 1
  skein *each* of black (310), pale old
  gold (677), light beige-gray (822),
  medium copper (920), and light
  antique blue (932)
Embroidery hoop, tapestry needle

INSTRUCTIONS
  Before beginning, see the general information on pages 180–183 for special cross-stitch tips and techniques,
and for materials necessary for working all counted cross-stitch projects.
  Chart pattern, *left*. On separate
graph, chart details. Use three plies of
floss and work the stitches over two
threads of fabric for most of the design. Stitch details using one ply of
floss one thread of fabric.
  Measure 4 inches down from the
top and 4 inches in from left side; begin upper-left corner of border here.

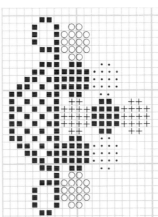

COLOR KEY
◫ **Dark Salmon (347)**
◉ **Dark Blue-Green (501)**
⊡ **Light Terra-Cotta (758)**
⊠ **Dark Hazelnut Brown (420)**
◢ **Medium Blue-Green (503)**
◼ **Black (310)**
⊞ **Pale Old Gold (677)**
◣ **Light Beige-Gray (822)**
▲ **Medium Copper (920)**
◿ **Light Antique Blue (932)**

Margret's Sampler

Wildlife Patterns From the World of Nature

Nature's graceful shapes, familiar motifs, and colors ranging from subtle to splashy lend themselves to many crafts, but are especially appealing in cross-stitches. The projects in this chapter include a sampler inspired by a day's visit to sun-dappled woods, and two smaller stitcheries, adaptations of this lovely design and personalized using the sampler alphabet.

A doe and her fawn are the focal points of the sampler, *opposite,* which features other interesting stitchery as well. The alphabet appears to be constructed of leafy twigs; and the oak leaf and acorn border consists of cross-stitches and backstitched outlines. Instructions begin on page 114.

batting, and trim the edge with piping.

A pattern for a photograph album like the one at *left* is a good introduction to designing cross-stitch. Because family names and album dimensions vary, you'll have to chart the name first.

Keeping the family name foremost, accent it with other elements, such as the oak leaf and acorn border designs. Keeping the stitch count of the fabric you intend to use in mind, plan the position of these other elements. For more on designing for cross-stitch, see pages 184 and 185.

S titching just the deer, fawn, and background foliage from the sampler on the preceding pages creates a smaller composition that you can use in a variety of ways. For example, you might embroider it on linen and frame it for a small wall hanging.

Or, create a picnic basket like the one *opposite*. Stitch the deer-and-fawn design with three-ply Persian yarn onto a creamy fabric. Then add your family's surname (or initials) to the area beneath it, using the alphabet from the sampler or any of the other alphabets in this book. Pad the stitchery with quilt

COLOR KEY

●	Dark Olive (263)	◣	Rust (326)
⊙	Medium Brown (351)	○	Light Rust (349)
▼	Light Green (243)	◪	Dark Brown (358)
⊠	Dark Green (246)	◩	Light Brown (369)
⬚	Light Olive (261)	·	Light Gray (397)
◹	Light Olive (261)		

▲	Dark Gray (400)		
■	Black (403)		
◤	Olive Drab (844)		
⊞	Gold (890)		

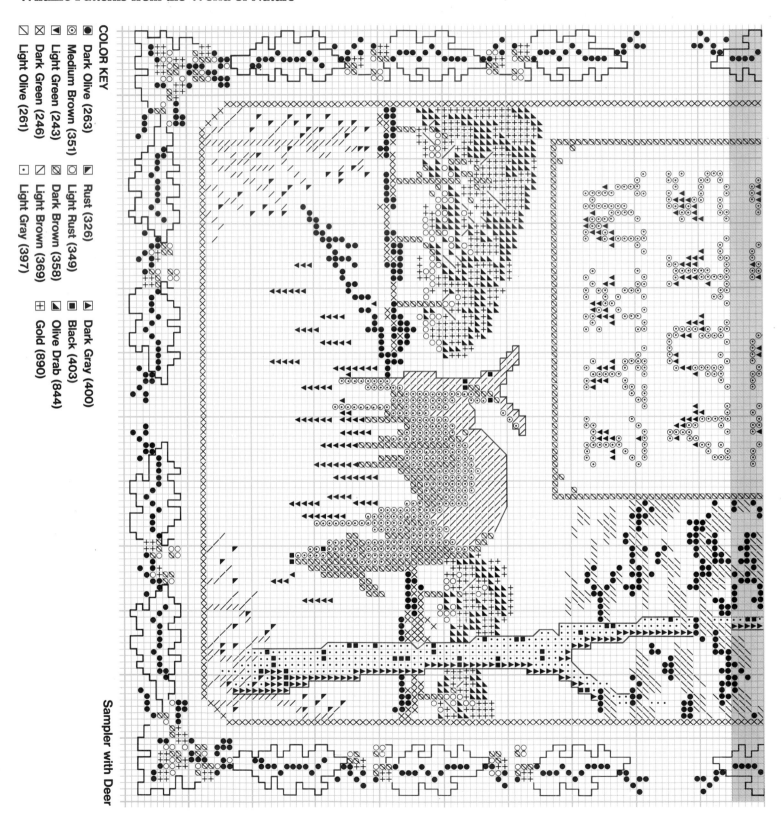

Sampler with Deer

114

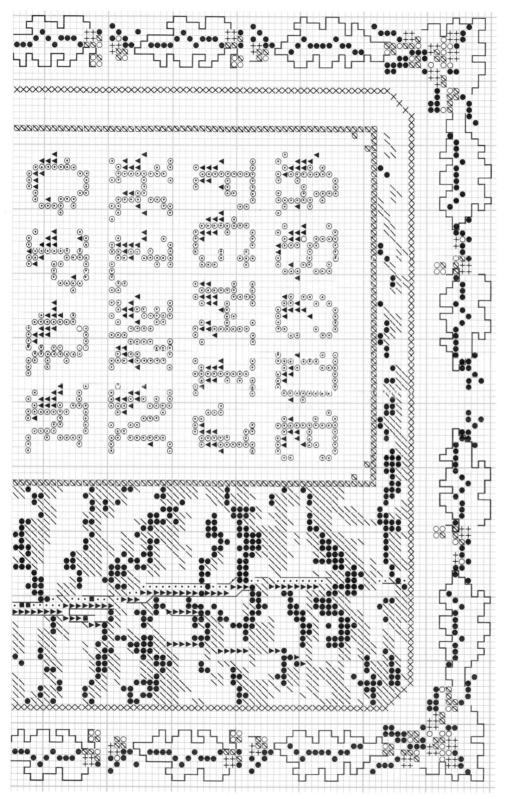

Sampler With Deer

Shown on pages 110–111.
Finished size of stitchery is 9⅜x13½ inches.
Design is 119 stitches wide and 169 stitches high.

MATERIALS
19x21-inch piece of beige 25-count Lugana fabric
Susan Bates Anchor embroidery floss: 2 skeins *each* of dark olive (263) and medium brown (351) and 1 skein *each* of light green (243), dark green (246), light olive (261), rust (326), light rust (349), dark brown (358), light brown (369), light gray (397), dark gray (400), black (403), olive drab (844), and gold (890)
Embroidery hoop, tapestry needle

INSTRUCTIONS
Before beginning, see the general information on pages 180–183 for special cross-stitch tips and techniques, and for materials necessary for working all counted cross-stitch projects.

Referring to pattern, *left,* chart design onto graph paper. Measure 4 inches down from top and 4 inches in from left of fabric piece. Begin stitching upper-left corner of border here. Use three plies of floss and work cross-stitches over two threads.

BACKSTITCHES: Outline large tree trunk in foreground using two plies of dark gray (400). Add branches to foliage in background using three plies of dark brown (358). Outline top edges of deer in medium brown (351). Outline oak leaves in border with three plies of dark olive (263).

Steam-press the stitchery on the wrong side.

Frame the sampler as desired.

Wildlife Patterns from the World of Nature

COLOR KEY

- ◉ Medium Fawn Brown (402)
- ◥ Light Olive Green (652)
- ◤ Medium Loden Green (692)
- ⊞ Old Gold (754)
- ◿ Light Fawn Brown (404)
- ◿ Dark Chocolate Brown (431)
- ● Dark Pine Green (661)
- ⊠ Dark Loden Green (691)
- ■ Black (220)
- ◤ Ginger (883)
- ◻ Light Ginger (884)

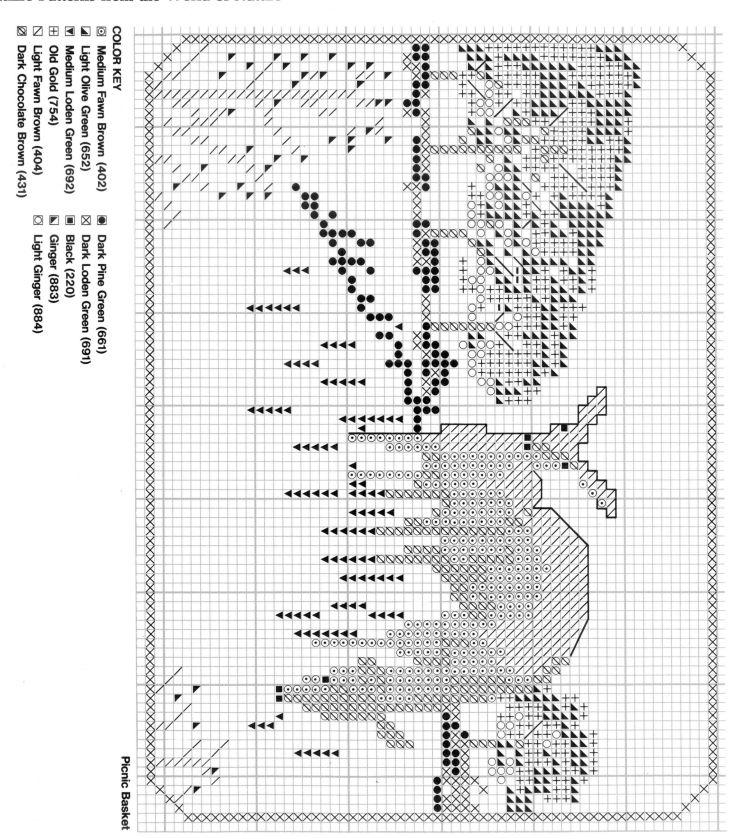

Picnic Basket

Picnic Basket

Shown on page 113.
Finished size of stitchery is approximately 9½x6¾ inches, excluding family name. Design is 85 stitches wide and 62 stitches high.

MATERIALS

18x18-inch piece of beige 18-count Davosa fabric
Paternayan 3-ply Persian yarn (32-inch lengths): 3 strands *each* of medium fawn brown (402), light olive green (652), medium loden green (692), and old gold (754); 2 strands *each* of light fawn brown (404), dark chocolate brown (431), dark pine green (661), and dark loden green (691); and 1 strand *each* of black (220), ginger (883), and light ginger (884)
Additional 3-ply Persian yarn in medium fawn brown (402) and medium loden green (692) for stitching family name
Picnic basket with hinged lid
18x36-inch piece of thick quilt batting
2 yards narrow piping, fabric glue
Transparent nylon sewing thread
Water-erasable marking pen
Embroidery hoop
Tapestry needle

INSTRUCTIONS

Before beginning, see the general information on pages 180–183 for special cross-stitch tips and techniques, and for materials necessary for working all counted cross-stitch projects.

Referring to pattern, *opposite,* chart design onto graph paper.

On a separate piece of graph paper chart family name using alphabet from Sampler with Deer (chart is on pages 114–115). Find and mark horizontal center of name.

Baste centers of Davosa fabric. Note horizontal and vertical centers of deer design. Using center lines as reference points, stitch design.

Stitch, using one strand of Persian yarn and working the cross-stitches over two threads of fabric.

To add family name below deer motif, baste a horizontal line 12 threads beneath border of deer motif. Using basted center line, horizontal center line of family name graph, stitch family name using medium fawn brown (402) and medium loden green (692). Align tops of letters with basted line on fabric.

Steam-press on the wrong side.

ASSEMBLY: Center and position stitchery on top of basket lid. With marker, trace exact lid shape on fabric, adding ¼ inch all around.

Cut batting into two 18x18-inch squares; set one square aside. Lay cross-stitch on top of one of the batting squares. Sew on traced outline.

With transparent nylon thread, machine-quilt around border of deer design. Hand-quilt around deer.

Sew piping to traced line. Trim batting to piping line. Cut out stitchery ½ inch beyond stitching line for piping. Press piping seam margin to wrong side. Topstitch through all layers with nylon thread close to piping.

Cut remaining batting square to lid shape, making outline ½ inch smaller all around. Glue smaller batting square to basket lid. Apply glue to wrong side of piping seam allowance and position in place atop basket.

Photograph Album

Shown on page 112.

MATERIALS

Even-weave fabric in color and stitch count desired
Embroidery floss or 3-ply Persian yarn
Photograph album
Fabric and piping for finishing
Quilt batting
Embroidery hoop
Tapestry needle

INSTRUCTIONS

Before beginning, see the general information on pages 180–183 for special cross-stitch tips and techniques, and for materials necessary for working all counted cross-stitch projects.

Refer to pages 184–185 for tips on designing cross-stitch patterns.

Determine finished size of stitchery for album cover; allow for fabric border around stitchery. Calculate number of available stitches for design by multiplying each dimension by the number of stitches per inch. For example, a 9x12-inch area to be stitched on 18-count even-weave fabric (over two threads) yields 81x108 stitches. On graph paper, outline an area that corresponds to these dimensions.

Referring to the pattern for the Sampler with Deer, pages 114–115, chart family name; add name to pattern.

After name is charted, add a border to the chart by using the oak leaf and acorn designs from the border of the sampler, or add any other motifs from the sampler as necessary.

ASSEMBLY: Remove cover from photograph album; measure height and width. Add borders and piping to stitchery so that it matches photograph album cover, plus ½ inch all around. Cut a piece of fabric for back of cover; if there are posts in cover, make machine buttonholes to accommodate hardware. Place right sides of stitchery and backing fabric together; stitch around three sides, turn, and slip over cover. Slip-stitch closed. Cover back of album to coordinate with covered front, if desired. Assemble album.

Woodland Blossoms

Capture the tender beauty of woodland wildflowers with this album of cross-stitch designs. The collection is based on a variety of flower patterns, such as violets, jack-in-the-pulpits, and trilliums.

Each of the Woodland Blossoms designs, including the white trillium, *above,* can stand alone or be incorporated into larger projects. For example, the guest towels on the chair, *far left,* feature one blossom and a border.

Instructions begin on page 126.

Select a favorite blossom from this sampler, *opposite,* to trim some towels like those at *right.* Stitching a single flower is a good way to become familiar with the designs before starting larger projects. Center the motif on a scrap of Aida cloth. Add one of the three border designs, edge the fabric with piping, and sew the Aida cloth to the towel.

The larger woodland flowers appear on the dramatic sampler, *opposite.* Yellow violets, a jack-in-the-pulpit, purple violets, red trillium, and white trillium are flanked by pairs of dogtooth violets and separated by grape hyacinth. Use the stately alphabet at the top of the sampler to personalize your cross-stitch projects. Accentuate the unusual horizontal shape of the design with the lower border stitches.

To duplicate the comb-painted frame, ask a frame shop to build one from clear white pine 1x4s. Paint the frame with semigloss enamel and let it dry. Then, paint the frame again, using a contrasting color. While the paint is wet, drag a piece of cardboard with notched edges across the painted surface.

The bed linens and shelf liners on these two pages illustrate how to use the woodland flower motifs creatively.

The bed skirt, *opposite*, fits a standard-length bed. A diamond pattern, stitched in Persian wool, frames each of the motifs. Large checks stitched in hues to match the blossoms add colorful accents above the diamonds. The blanket edging, *opposite*, is designed to fit any woven blanket and is an adaptation of the bed skirt.

The shelf liners, *right*, can be custom-made to fit any cabinet. Select as many of the blossom motifs as you wish and stitch them on strips of even-weave fabric.

ines of wild roses trail across these room accessories. They're all based on a semicircular motif of wild rose blossoms, hips, and leaves.

The pair of pillows, *left,* uses the motif in two striking ways. The pattern for the larger rectangular pillow calls for repeating the motif 16 times to form a serpentine border around the pillow top. The smaller pillow features a circular motif of wild roses surrounded by four additional motifs.

To finish the pillows, select striped and plaid fabrics in colors that complement the stitcheries. Then, use one for piping and the other for ruffles on each pillow. See pages 186 and 187 for more on finishing pillows.

A box designed for a needlework insert, such as the one *above,* is ideal for displaying a ring of wild roses. Stitch just the center ring of the small pillow, *left;* then personalize it by adding a letter from the sampler inside the ring, if you wish.

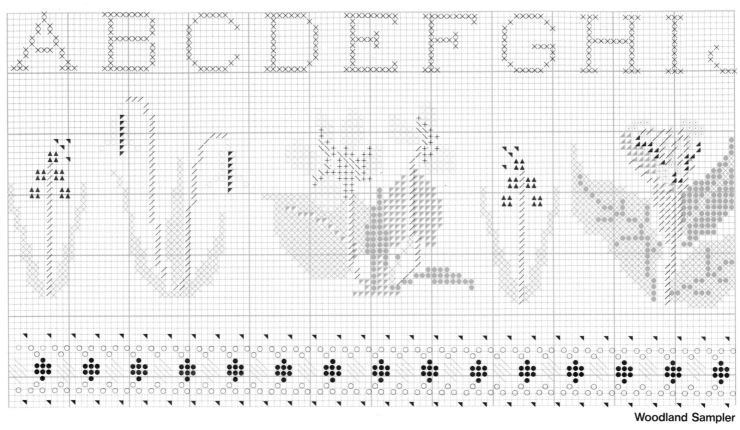

Woodland Sampler

COLOR KEY

- ◉ Coral (351)
- ◺ Pale Mahogany (402)
- ⊠ Medium Gray-Green (3052)
- ⊠ Medium Yellow-Green (3347)
- ⊡ White
- ◤ Dark Periwinkle Blue (333)
- ▲ Periwinkle Blue (340)

- ◣ Dark Salmon (347)
- ⊙ Medium Terra-Cotta (356)
- ▽ Light Blue-Green (504)
- ■ Medium Violet (553)
- ◺ Light Violet (554)
- ▣ Dark Moss Green (580)
- ⊞ Light Old Gold (676)

- ▣ Light Christmas Green (701)
- ⊙ Plum (718)
- ▢ Medium Olive Green (733)
- ▢ Medium Yellow (743)
- ◤ Pale Yellow (745)
- ◺ Dark Plum (915)
- ◪ Dark Red-Copper (918)

- ◎ Medium Avocado Green (937)
- ◿ Light Nile Green (955)
- ⊞ Light Pumpkin (970)
- ▢ Pale Beaver Gray (3072)
- ◥ Black-Brown (3371)

Sampler

Shown on page 121.
Finished size is 40x7¼ inches.
Design is 360 stitches wide
and 66 stitches high.

MATERIALS
50x18-inch piece of light gray 18-count
 Davosa fabric
DMC embroidery floss: 2 skeins *each*
 of coral (351), pale mahogany
(402), dark green (937), medium
gray-green (3052), and medium
yellow-green (3347) and 1 skein
each of white, dark periwinkle
blue (333), periwinkle blue (340),
dark salmon (347), medium terra-
cotta (356), light blue-green (504),
medium violet (553), light violet
(554), dark moss green (580), light
old gold (676), light Christmas
green (701), plum (718), medium
olive green (733), medium yellow
(743), pale yellow (745), dark plum
(915), dark red-copper (918),
medium avocado green (937), light
nile green (955), light pumpkin
(970), pale beaver gray (3072), and
black-brown (3371)
Embroidery hoop
Tapestry needle

INSTRUCTIONS
 Before beginning, see the general information on pages 180–183 for special cross-stitch tips and techniques,
and for materials necessary for work-

Woodland Sampler

COLOR KEY

- ◉ Coral (351)
- ◹ Pale Mahogany (402)
- ⊠ Medium Gray-Green (3052)
- ⊠ Medium Yellow-Green (3347)
- ⊡ White
- ◥ Dark Periwinkle Blue (333)
- ▲ Periwinkle Blue (340)

- ◤ Dark Salmon (347)
- ⊡ Medium Terra-Cotta (356)
- ▽ Light Blue-Green (504)
- ■ Medium Violet (553)
- ◹ Light Violet (554)
- ▣ Dark Moss Green (580)
- ⊞ Light Old Gold (676)

- ◐ Light Christmas Green (701)
- ⊙ Plum (718)
- ◪ Medium Olive Green (733)
- ◻ Medium Yellow (743)
- ◤ Pale Yellow (745)
- ◺ Dark Plum (915)
- ◩ Dark Red-Copper (918)

- ◎ Medium Avocado Green (937)
- ◪ Light Nile Green (955)
- ⊞ Light Pumpkin (970)
- ◷ Pale Beaver Gray (3072)
- ◣ Black-Brown (3371)

ing all counted cross-stitch projects. Referring to patterns, pages 126–128, chart design onto graph paper with markers. Tape together several sheets of graph paper, if necessary.

Stitch, using four plies of floss and working the cross-stitches over two threads of fabric.

Measure 5 inches down from the top and 5 inches in from the left side; begin stitching upper-left corner of sampler here. Mount fabric in hoop and cross-stitch all letters, flower mo-tifs, and border from left to right.

Wash stitchery, if necessary, and steam-press on the wrong side.

Frame the sampler as desired.

Shelf Liners

Shown on page 123.
Finished depth is 4¾ inches.

MATERIALS

For each liner

7-inch-wide length of light gray 14-count Aida cloth as long as shelf plus 1 inch

DMC embroidery floss: See charts and instructions for the sampler, beginning on page 126, for colors; amounts of floss used depend upon motifs selected from the sampler

Materials for piping

Embroidery hoop, tapestry needle

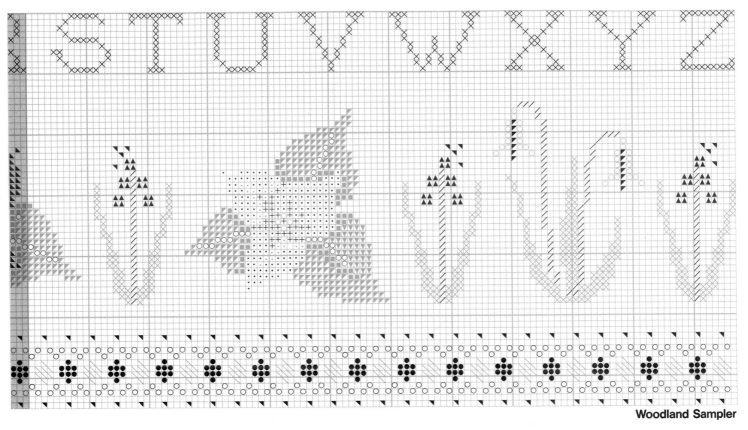

Woodland Sampler

COLOR KEY

- ◉ **Coral (351)**
- ◩ **Pale Mahogany (402)**
- ⊠ **Medium Gray-Green (3052)**
- ⊠ **Medium Yellow-Green (3347)**
- ⊡ **White**
- ◣ **Dark Periwinkle Blue (333)**
- ▲ **Periwinkle Blue (340)**

- ◣ **Dark Salmon (347)**
- ⊙ **Medium Terra-Cotta (356)**
- ▼ **Light Blue-Green (504)**
- ■ **Medium Violet (553)**
- ◿ **Light Violet (554)**
- ▦ **Dark Moss Green (580)**
- ⊞ **Light Old Gold (676)**

- ◉ **Light Christmas Green (701)**
- ⊙ **Plum (718)**
- ◿ **Medium Olive Green (733)**
- ▢ **Medium Yellow (743)**
- ◤ **Pale Yellow (745)**
- ◹ **Dark Plum (915)**
- ◿ **Dark Red-Copper (918)**

- ◎ **Medium Avocado Green (937)**
- ◿ **Light Nile Green (955)**
- ⊞ **Light Pumpkin (970)**
- ⊡ **Pale Beaver Gray (3072)**
- ◢ **Black-Brown (3371)**

INSTRUCTIONS

Before beginning, see the general information on pages 180–183 for special cross-stitch tips and techniques, and for materials necessary for working all counted cross-stitch projects.

Plan finished width of shelf liner; calculate number of stitches needed to span shelf width by multiplying width in inches by 14. (For example, a 30-inch-wide shelf will accommodate 420 stitches.)

Using pattern for the sampler, pages 126–128, and graph paper, chart combinations of flowers as desired. See photograph on page 123 for ideas. Add border designs from pattern, *opposite,* leaving seven threads between bottom of flowers and top of border.

Using two plies of floss, work the cross-stitches over one thread of fabric. When stitching is completed, machine-zigzag-stitch along bottom edge to prevent raveling.

Make piping according to general instructions, pages 186–187. Pin and sew piping to bottom edge, using ¼-inch seams; press raw edges toward top. Stitch ¼-inch hem along top edge and sides.

Press a fold 2 inches down from the top edge, wrong sides together. Align this pressed fold with the edge of the shelf so that the stitchery hangs down; secure in place with tacks or double-faced tape.

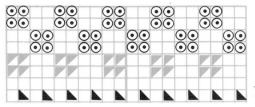

Border A
COLOR KEY
⊙ Plum (718)
▨ Medium Olive Green (733)
◣ Dark Salmon (347)

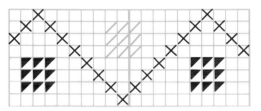

Border B
COLOR KEY
⊠ Medium Gray-Green (3052)
☐ Violet (554)
▰ Pale Yellow (745)

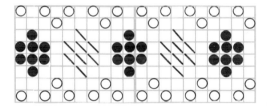

Border C
COLOR KEY
◉ Medium Avocado Green (937)
⬤ Coral (351)
◨ Pale Mahogany (402)

Guest Towels

Shown on page 120.

MATERIALS
Fingertip towels
5-inch-wide strips of 14-count Aida cloth as long as width of towels plus 1 inch
DMC embroidery floss: See charts and instructions for sampler, beginning on page 126, for colors

Materials for piping
Embroidery hoop
Tapestry needle

INSTRUCTIONS
Before beginning, see the general information on pages 180–183 for special cross-stitch tips and techniques, and for materials necessary for working all counted cross-stitch projects.

Baste horizontal and vertical center of fabric. Stitch a single-flower motif from sampler in center. Use two plies of floss and work the cross-stitches over one thread of fabric. Stitch a border motif (see charts, *left*) along horizontal center (leaving one stitch free between motif and border) of fabric strip. Press stitchery on wrong side.

Make piping according to general instructions, pages 186–187. Pin piping to top and bottom edge of fabric about ½ inch from flower; sew in place. Trim excess fabric and fold to wrong side. Topstitch fabric to towel. Fold under short ends of Aida cloth twice; blindstitch.

Press stitcheries lightly on wrong side of towel.

Blanket Edging

Shown on page 122.
Design is 79 stitches high.

MATERIALS
Woven blanket
12-inch-wide piece of light gray 18-count Davosa fabric, as long as width of blanket plus 8 inches
DMC embroidery floss: See charts and instructions for sampler, beginning on page 126, for colors; amounts will vary according to motifs used
Paternayan 3-ply Persian yarn (32-inch lengths): 25 strands *each* of grape (312) and golden brown (440)

Polyester fleece cut to same size as Davosa fabric
Fabric for lining and piping
Embroidery hoop, tapestry needle

INSTRUCTIONS
Before beginning, see the general information on pages 180–183 for special cross-stitch tips and techniques, and for materials necessary for working all counted cross-stitch projects.

Plan border to fit blanket; each multiple of the pointed border measures 9 inches across. Divide the width of the blanket by nine to determine number of points possible for edging. (For example, an 80-inch-wide blanket will require a 72-inch-wide edging.) The remaining width of the blanket will be trimmed away later.

Measure in 4 inches from the edge and 6 inches down from the top of the Davosa fabric. Using the pattern, page 130, begin stitching sawtooth edging in three-ply Persian yarn. Use one ply of Persian and work the cross-stitches over two threads of fabric. Repeat the pattern until the correct number of points have been worked.

Stitch the upper border using scraps of three-ply Persian yarn.

Using patterns from the sampler, chart seven motifs on graph paper. Combine more than one of the smaller motifs (grape hyacinth and dogtooth violets) to fit within a square. Stitch a flower motif in each point. Use four plies of floss and work the cross-stitches over two threads.

Steam-press the stitchery on the wrong side.

ASSEMBLY: Make piping, if desired (see general directions, pages 186–187). Baste stitchery to fleece; cut a piece of backing fabric to same size.

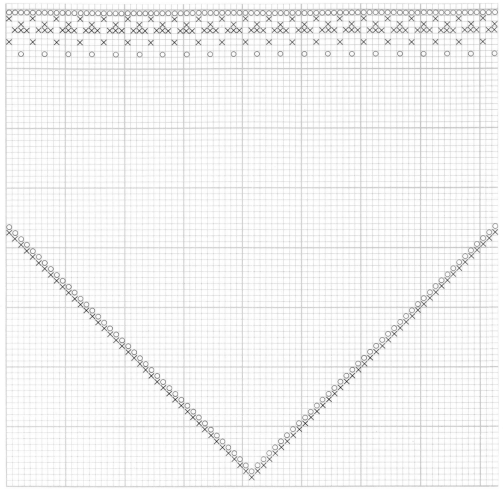

COLOR KEY

▢ Grape (312)   ⊠ Golden Brown (440)

DMC embroidery floss: See charts and instructions for sampler, beginning on page 126, for colors; amounts will vary according to flower motifs included

Paternayan 3-ply Persian yarn (32-inch lengths): 10 strands *each* of grape (312) and golden brown (440)

80x12-inch piece of polyester fleece

2½ yards coordinating fabric for backing and piping

Muslin or old sheet

INSTRUCTIONS

Note: The bed skirt shown is designed for a twin- or full-size bed, and works best for a bed with both headboard and footboard. The skirt is attached to a fabric panel and inserted between the mattress and box spring.

Before beginning, see the general information on pages 180–183 for special cross-stitch tips and techniques, and for materials necessary for working all counted cross-stitch projects.

The pattern, *opposite,* represents one section of bed skirt. Measure 5 inches down from top and 4 inches in from left end of fabric. Begin stitching the border here, starting at upper-left corner of pattern. Use one ply of Persian yarn and work the cross-stitches over two threads of fabric.

Repeat the border section for a total of eight times—there will be seven complete squares and a half-square at each end.

Using patterns from the sampler, beginning on page 126, chart seven motifs on graph paper. Combine more than one of the smaller motifs (grape hyacinth and dogtooth violets). Stitch a flower motif in each square. Use four plies of floss and work the cross-stitches over two threads.

Using scraps of floss in colors desired, stitch nine-square checkerboard motifs in half-squares above and at the end of the row of squares.

If bed is seen from both sides, make

Machine-stitch a line ¼ inch past Persian yarn around points and upper borders, and along short edges. Measure stitching line past center of outer row of stitches.

Stitch piping to this line, easing in and around points. Trim fleece to ⅛ inch past stitching; clip corners. Place right sides of backing fabric and stitchery together. Stitch around piping line again. Trim backing; clip corners, turn, and press lightly.

Cut down width of blanket, if necessary, to match width of edging. Finish edges.

Place right sides of stitchery and blanket together. Stitch together, sewing through stitchery and fleece. Press raw edges of stitchery and fleece and edge of blanket up toward points. Turn under raw edge of backing fabric and blindstitch closed.

Bed Skirt

Shown on page 122.
Design is 81 stitches high.

MATERIALS
For a twin- or full-size bed
Two 80x15-inch pieces of light gray 18-count Davosa fabric

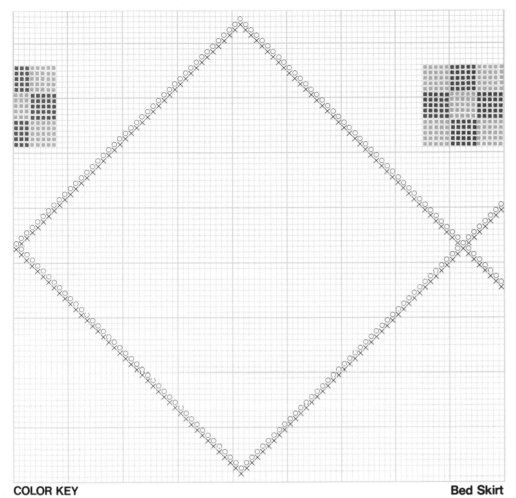

COLOR KEY

☐ Grape (312)   ☒ Golden Brown (440)

Bed Skirt

Wild Rose
Rectangular Pillow

Shown on page 124.
Finished size is 24x21 inches,
including ruffle.
Design is 224 stitches wide
and 190 stitches high.

MATERIALS

26x24-inch piece of khaki 14-count
   Aida cloth
DMC embroidery floss: 1 skein *each*
   of white, dark coral (349), medium
   terra-cotta (356), coral (351), light
   Christmas green (701), medium
   yellow (743), medium yellow-green
   (3347), and black-brown (3371)
Fabric for backing, piping, and ruffle
18½x16-inch pillow or fiberfill for
   stuffing
Embroidery hoop
Tapestry needle

INSTRUCTIONS

Before beginning, see the general information on pages 180–183 for special cross-stitch tips and techniques,
and for materials necessary for working all counted cross-stitch projects.

The pattern, pages 132–133, is a position diagram for pillow top. The pattern, page 133, is a stitch diagram for
each of the 16 pattern repeats used for
the pillow top. Chart entire pillow top
on graph paper before beginning, using position diagram for placing semicircular rose motif on pillow. Chart
WELCOME (using letters from sampler) and stripes above and below lettering in center. Or, chart a family
name, verse, or other sentiment in pillow center.

Stitch, using two plies of floss and
working the cross-stitches over one
thread of fabric.

another panel for other side of bed, if
desired.

Steam-press the stitchery on wrong
side.

ASSEMBLY: Make piping, if desired.
Baste stitchery to fleece; cut a piece of
backing fabric to same size.

Machine-stitch a line ¼ inch past
Persian yarn border (measure from
center of outer row of stitches). Stitch
piping to this line and along short
edges of stitchery panel, easing in and
around points. Trim fleece to ⅛ inch

past stitching; clip corners. Place right
sides of backing fabric and stitchery
together. Stitch around piping line
again; trim backing, clip corners, turn,
and press lightly.

From muslin, piece together sufficient yardage to cover box spring (or
cut panel from a sheet). Make panel
as long as assembled skirt, and add
½-inch seam allowances on the side
edges. Place right sides of muslin assembly and stitchery together. Stitch
along long edge with ½-inch seams.
Open, press seams toward muslin;
topstitch just above seam. Add ruffled
underskirt in a contrasting fabric beneath bed skirt, if desired.

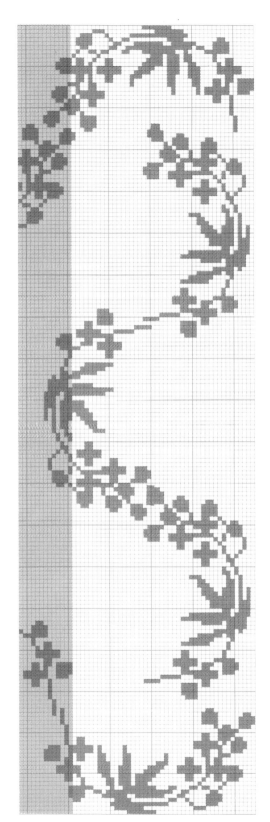

Rectangular Wild Rose Pillow

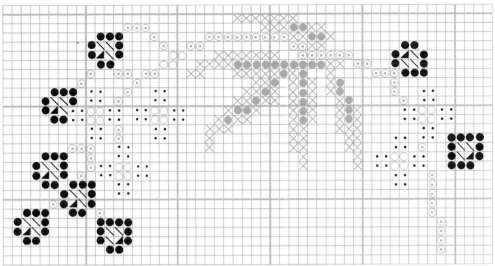

COLOR KEY
- ⊡ White
- ◉ Dark Coral (349)
- ⊡ Medium Terra-Cotta (356)
- ◫ Coral (351)
- ▦ Light Christmas Green (701)
- ☐ Medium Yellow (743)
- ⊠ Medium Yellow-Green (3347)
- ◪ Black-Brown (3371)

Measure 4 inches down from the top and 4 inches in from left side; begin stitching upper-left corner of border here. Mount fabric in hoop and start cross-stitching with upper-left border.

When stitchery is completed, steam-press on the wrong side.

See general directions on pages 186–187 for completing a pillow.

Wild Rose Round Pillow

Shown on page 125.
Finished diameter is 14 inches, including ruffle.
Design is 97 stitches wide and 97 stitches high.

MATERIALS
14x14-inch piece of khaki 14-count Aida cloth
DMC embroidery floss: 1 skein *each* of white, dark coral (349), medium terra-cotta (356), coral (351), light Christmas green (701), medium yellow (743), medium yellow-green (3347), and black-brown (3371)
10-inch-diameter pillow form
Fabric for backing, ruffle, and piping
Embroidery hoop
Tapestry needle

INSTRUCTIONS
Before beginning, see the general information on pages 180–183 for special cross-stitch tips and techniques, and for materials necessary for working all counted cross-stitch projects.

Refer to the pattern, page 34; note horizontal and vertical centers. Baste horizontal and vertical centers of fabric. Use these lines as reference points when stitching design.

Use two plies of floss and work the cross-stitches over one thread of fabric to stitch design.

See general instructions on pages 186–187 for completing a pillow.

Woodland Blossoms

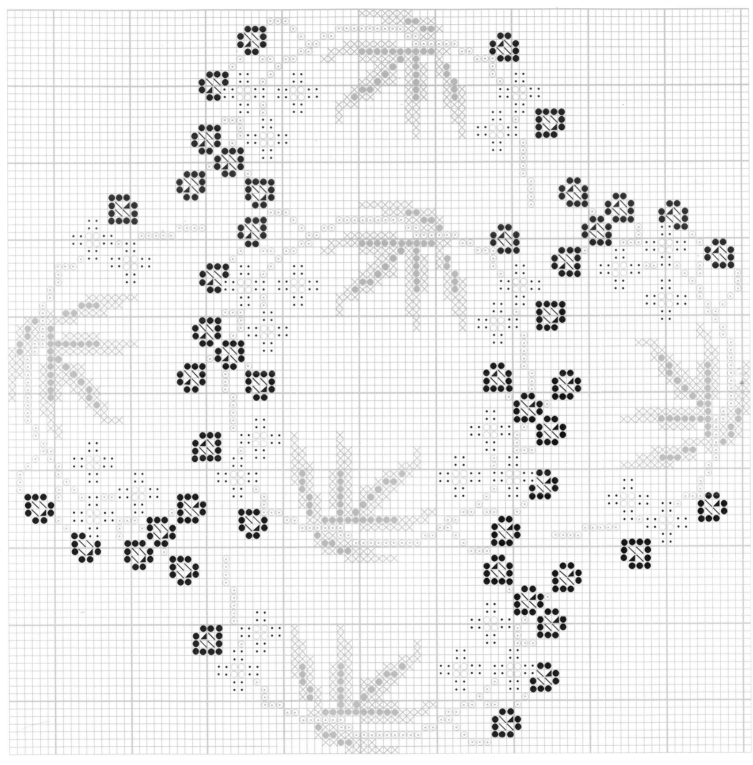

COLOR KEY

- ⊡ White
- ◉ Dark Coral (349)
- ◉ Medium Terra-Cotta (356)
- ◺ Coral (351)
- ◉ Light Christmas Green (701)
- ☐ Medium Yellow (743)
- ⊠ Medium Yellow-Green (3347)
- ◢ Black-Brown (3371)

Wild Rose Box-Lid Insert

Shown on page 125.
Finished diameter is 3¾ inches.

MATERIALS
Wooden box with lid designed to receive needlework
8x8-inch piece of ecru 14-count Aida cloth
DMC embroidery floss: 1 skein *each* of white, dark coral (349), medium terra-cotta (356), coral (351), light Christmas green (701), medium yellow (743), medium yellow-green (3347), and black-brown (3371)
Scrap of quilt batting
Embroidery hoop
Tapestry needle

INSTRUCTIONS
Before beginning, see the general information on pages 180–183 for special cross-stitch tips and techniques, and for materials necessary for working all counted cross-stitch projects.

Refer to pattern for Wild Rose Round Pillow, *opposite;* note horizontal and vertical centers. Baste horizontal and vertical centers of fabric. Use these lines as reference points when stitching design.

Stitch only center circle of wild roses. Use two plies of floss and work the cross-stitches over one thread of fabric.

If desired, add an initial or monogram in center of wild rose motif. Use a capital letter from the sampler (charts begin on page 126), or any of the other alphabet styles in this book.

Press stitchery on wrong side. Pad stitchery with quilt batting, and mount into box lid according to manufacturer's instructions.

Patchwork Pillow

Shown on page 118.
Finished size is 15x18 inches, excluding ruffle.

MATERIALS
Scraps of light gray 18-count Davosa fabric
DMC embroidery floss: See charts and instructions for sampler, beginning on page 126, for colors of the following motifs: purple violet, yellow violet, jack-in-the-pulpit, red trillium, and white trillium
⅓ yard of light gray corduroy to match Davosa fabric
Fabric for backing, piping, ruffle
2 yards cording
Polyester fiberfill
Water-erasable marking pen, ruler
Embroidery hoop
Tapestry needle

INSTRUCTIONS
Before beginning, see the general information on pages 180–183 for special cross-stitch tips and techniques, and for materials necessary for working all counted cross-stitch projects.

Referring to the pattern for the sampler, pages 126–128, chart purple violet, yellow violet, jack-in-the-pulpit, red trillium, and white trillium on graph paper. Use four plies of floss and stitch each motif on a scrap of fabric, working the cross-stitches over two threads.

Centering each motif, mark finished sizes of stitcheries with marking pen; finished size of purple violet is 5x8 inches and finished size of remaining stitcheries is 5x5 inches. Mark cutting line ½ inch past finished sizes; zigzag-stitch along cutting lines. Cut out the stitcheries and set aside.

Note: For assembly, use ½-inch seams unless otherwise indicated.

From corduroy, cut four 2x6-inch strips and six 2x9-inch strips on the lengthwise grain. Cut six 2x6-inch strips and four 2x9-inch strips on the crosswise grain.

Referring to photograph, page 118, sew together five strips of each length, alternating grain. Press seams open.

Piece stitcheries and corduroy assemblies together in horizontal rows. Join two cross-stitched squares to each end of a 6x9-inch pieced rectangle to make the top and bottom rows. Join two pieced corduroy squares to ends of purple violet stitchery to make the center row. Press all seams open.

Join rows, matching seams carefully. Press seams open.

Refer to general directions, pages 186–187, for completing a pillow.

Note: You can use the Woodland Blossoms motifs—or any other motif in this book—to create a variety of patchwork pillows. One simple way to create a patchwork pillow is to begin with a stitched motif—a flower design, monogram, or even an entire alphabet. Then, using patchwork instruction and pattern books as a guide, add pieced borders around center motif and complete the pillow according to the general directions, pages 186–187. Select patchwork fabrics to coordinate with background fabric and colors of floss used.

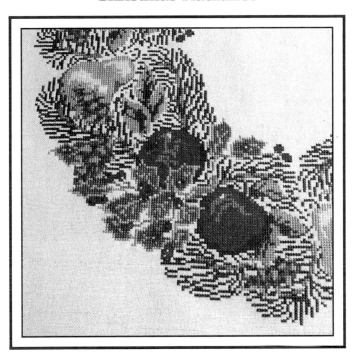

Holiday Cross-Stitch For Trims, Table, and Tree

The warmest and most inviting decorations in any festive holiday home are sure to be those that are made by hand. Our collection of Christmas cross-stitch projects contains beautiful designs for all skill levels—from quick-and-easy ornaments that you can make in an evening to heirloom projects that you will treasure forever.

Inspired by wreaths of evergreen branches adorned with fruit, the Della Robbia tablecloth, *opposite,* is a tribute to a skilled stitcher's talents. The wreath is based on a quadrant pattern and features pears, apples, and pinecones nestled in pine and holly boughs.

Instructions and charts for the projects shown in this chapter begin on page 146.

Special touches like the unique ornaments and stocking shown here provide great focal points for trimming the tree and decorating stairways and mantels.

The festive alphabet, *left,* is cleverly arranged to form an outline of a Christmas tree. The "tree," worked over one thread of fabric, is ideal for an ornament. Or, stitch it over two or more threads to create a wall hanging or pillow top.

The "Noel" ornament and stocking, *opposite,* echo the motifs of the wreath stitchery on the two preceding pages.

A realistic pinecone and a few snippets of greenery make up the design on the front of the ornament. Try personalizing the ornament by adding a family name or initials instead of the greeting.

Another adaptation of the fruit and foliage motifs embellishes the front of the elegant stocking. The dramatic placement of the stitchery along one side of the stocking emphasizes the graceful lines and shapes.

E very Christmas tree deserves to have at least one cross-stitch ornament brighten its branches. The designs on these two pages work up so quickly that it's easy to make one or several in time for this year's tree-trimming party.

The ornaments, *opposite,* are nothing more than geometric borders with greetings of the season stitched in the centers. In addition to greetings, use family members' names, special dates, or other sentiments. Or, use a more finely woven fabric than that shown here, and work the border over two threads. Then, stitch a short poem or lyrics from a Christmas carol over just one thread.

The ornaments, *above,* are stitched from quadrant patterns to form medallions. Adjust the colors of the motifs, if desired, to set off your decor. (Any combination of a half-dozen or so colors is all you need to stitch the geometric motif.) Either choice is a good way to use up leftover floss and even-weave fabrics.

One-of-a-kind accessories like these table decorations are sure to be treasured from year to year.

The square mat, *opposite,* not only features a festive repeat pattern around its edges, but is shaped and fringed. Making a line of stitches above the fringe prevents raveling.

The doilies, *above,* also are trimmed with symbols of the season. Both are stitched from a quadrant pattern and finished in a circle.

Beautiful borders worked in cross-stitch are among the most versatile of needlework designs.

The stocking and towels, *above,* share a simple border design that's used for maximum effect. For the stocking, a poinsettia design is centered across the cuff and a pair of names personalizes the trim.

The guest towels begin with linens specially designed with even-weave bands along the short ends so that no finishing work is required.

The picture, *opposite,* offers a cheery welcome for holiday guests. Hang it in an entry or wherever visitors gather in your home.

The picture's design contains several motifs and patterns that lend themselves to other projects as well. For example, the top section is just right for a greeting card for someone special. Try using the cabin and trees segment for an ornament, or the holly leaf border along the edge of some napkins for the Christmas dinner table.

Christmas Greetings

Christmas Greetings

FROM OUR HOME
TO YOURS

Christmas Greetings

Holiday Cross-Stitch for Trims, Table, and Tree

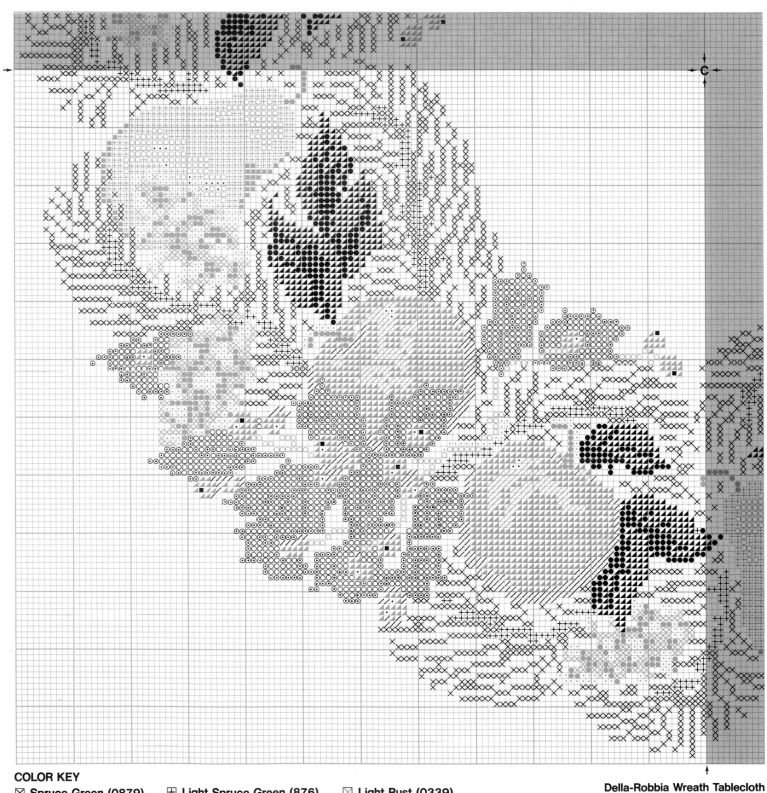

C

Della-Robbia Wreath Tablecloth

COLOR KEY

⊠ Spruce Green (0879)	⊞ Light Spruce Green (876)	⊠ Light Rust (0339)
◪ Red (019)	⬗ Dark Red (020)	◉ Pale Yellow (301)
⊙ Pale Olive (945)	⊞ Deep Yellow (306)	▨ Gold (309)	◢ Light Avocado (265)
● Avocado (269)	⊡ Tan (347)	◯ Light Brown (0833)	⊡ White (402)
◯ Blue-Green (211)	▨ Medium Brown (357)	◹ Light Red (010)	◼ Black (403)

Della Robbia Wreath Tablecloth

Shown on pages 136–137.
Finished diameter of stitchery is approximately 21 inches.

MATERIALS
64x64-inch piece of white hardanger
Susan Bates Anchor embroidery
  floss: 6 skeins of spruce green
  (879); 4 skeins of red (19); 3 skeins
  each of pale olive (945), avocado
  (269), blue-green (211); 2 skeins
  each of light spruce green (876),
  dark red (20), deep yellow (306),
  tan (347), medium brown (357),
  light rust (339); and 1 skein *each*
  of pale yellow (301), gold (309),
  light brown (833), light red (10),
  light avocado (265), white (402),
  and black (403)
Embroidery hoop, tapestry needle

INSTRUCTIONS
Before beginning, see the general information on pages 180–183 for special cross-stitch tips and techniques, and for materials necessary for working all counted cross-stitch projects.

The pattern, *opposite,* is a quadrant of complete design. Use graph paper and colored pencils or felt-tip markers to chart one-fourth of wreath design. Note horizontal and vertical centers.

Baste horizontal and vertical centers of fabric. Using center lines of pattern and basted lines on fabric as reference points, stitch lower-left fourth of wreath. Use three plies of floss and work cross-stitches over two threads of fabric. Rotate chart one quarter-turn clockwise to stitch upper-left quarter of wreath. (*Note:* The pattern shows an overlap of 10 stitches past the center line to aid in aligning the pattern as it is turned.) Continue in this manner until wreath is finished. Steam-press stitchery on wrong side. Finish tablecloth with a rolled hem to diameter desired.

Sampler Tree Ornament

Shown on page 138.
Finished size is 5x7 inches.
Design is 64 stitches wide and 104 stitches high.

MATERIALS
For each ornament
8x10-inch piece of white 18-count
  Aida cloth
DMC embroidery floss: 1 skein *each*
  of green (561), olive (731), dark red
  (326), navy (336), and rose (335)

Fabric for finishing
Fiberfill
Embroidery hoop, tapestry needle

INSTRUCTIONS
Before beginning, see the general information on pages 180–183 for special cross-stitch tips and techniques, and for materials necessary for working all counted cross-stitch projects.

Referring to the pattern, page 148, chart design on graph paper. Note horizontal and vertical centers. Baste horizontal and vertical centers on Aida cloth. Using center lines of pattern and basted lines on fabric as reference points, stitch design. Use two plies of floss and work the cross-stitches over one thread of fabric.

See general directions on pages 186–187 for completing an ornament.

Holly Ornament

COLOR KEY
◩ **Red (019)**
◨ **Dark Red (020)**
◉ **Pale Olive (945)**
◎ **Blue-Green (211)**
⊞ **Light Spruce Green (0876)**
⊠ **Spruce Green (0879)**

⊡ **Tan (347)**
◻ **Light Brown (0883)**
▣ **Medium Brown (357)**
⊠ **Light Rust (0339)**
◼ **Black**
⊡ **White**

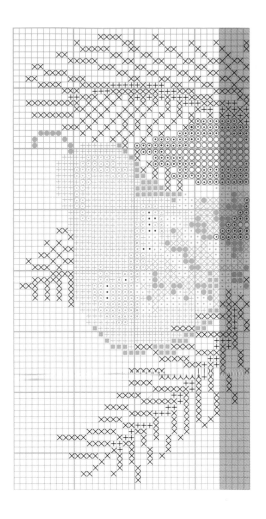

Shown on page 139.

Holly Ornament

*Shown on page 139.
Finished size is 7x5 inches.
Design is 76x54 stitches.*

MATERIALS
For each ornament
9x7-inch piece of white hardanger
Susan Bates Anchor embroidery
  floss: 1 skein *each* of red (19),
  dark red (20), pale olive (945),
  blue-green (211), light spruce green
  (876), spruce green (879), tan (347),
  light brown (883), medium brown
  (357), light rust (339), black, and
  white
Fabric for finishing, fiberfill
Embroidery hoop, tapestry needle

COLOR KEY

Sampler Tree Ornament

◎	Deep Rose (326)
⊡	Rose (335)
●	Navy Blue (336)
⊠	Dark Sea Foam Green (561)
⊞	Dark Olive Green (731)

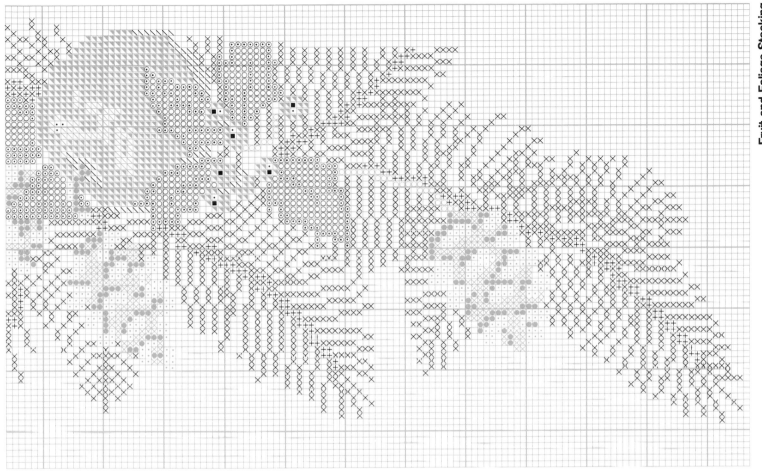

⊠ Spruce Green (879)
⊡ Pale Yellow (301)
⊞ Deep Yellow (306)
▨ Gold (309)
☐ Tan (347)
▢ Light Brown (883)
▨ Medium Brown (357)
⊠ Light Rust (339)
⊚ Pale Olive (945)
⊘ Blue-Green (211)
⊞ Light Spruce Green (876)
◪ Light Red (10)
◪ Red (19)
◪ Dark Red (20)
▣ Black
⊡ White

INSTRUCTIONS

Before beginning, see the general information on pages 180–183 for special cross-stitch tips and techniques, and for materials necessary for working all counted cross-stitch projects.

Referring to the pattern, page 147, chart design on graph paper. Note horizontal and vertical centers. Baste horizontal and vertical centers on hardanger. Using center lines of pattern and basted lines on fabric as reference points, stitch design. Use three plies of floss and work the cross-stitches over two threads of the fabric.

See general directions on pages 186–187 for completing an ornament.

Fruit-and-Foliage Stocking

Shown on page 139.
Finished size is 12x20 inches.
Design is 73 stitches wide and 155 stitches high.

MATERIALS

15x24-inch piece of white hardanger Susan Bates Anchor embroidery
floss: 2 skeins of spruce green (879); 1 skein *each* of pale yellow (301), deep yellow (306), gold (309), tan (347), light brown (883), medium brown (357), light rust (339), pale olive (945), blue-green (211), light spruce green (876), light

red (10), red (19), dark red (20), black, and white
Fabric for backing, lining, and piping
1 yard polyester fleece
2 yards cable cord
Embroidery hoop, tapestry needle

INSTRUCTIONS

Before beginning, see the general information on pages 180–183 for special cross-stitch tips and techniques, and for materials necessary for working all counted cross-stitch projects.

Referring to the pattern, pages 148–149, chart design onto graph paper.

Use three plies of floss and work the cross-stitches over two threads of fabric.

Measure 4 inches down from the top and 4 inches in from the right; begin stitching top of stocking here.

Steam-press on wrong side.

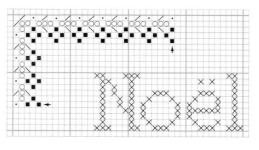

Stocking Pattern
1-Square = 1-Inch

ASSEMBLY: Enlarge stocking pattern, *below*. Baste stitchery and backing fabric to pieces of fleece. Outline stocking shape on the stitchery with water-erasable marking pen. Place wrong sides of backing and front together. Cut out, adding a ½-inch seam allowance. Place right sides of two pieces of lining fabric together; cut out to same shape as stocking front.

Cover cord with fabric for piping.

Sew piping to front along outline, omitting top edge. Place right sides of front and back together; stitch along piping line. Trim seam allowance to ¼ inch; clip curves.

With right sides facing, stitch lining pieces together with a ½-inch seam, leaving an 8-inch opening along long edge for turning.

Sew piping along top edge of front and back, overlapping at back edge. Place top edges of lining and stocking

assembly together, right sides facing, and stitch along piping line. Trim seam allowance to ¼ inch; clip curves. Turn stocking through lining; turn lining and slip-stitch closed. Tuck lining into stocking and tack at toe. Press. Topstitch around top edge.

Seasonal-Sayings Ornaments

Shown on page 140.
Finished size of each ornament is 5x2¾ inches.
Design is 55 stitches wide and 31 stitches high.

MATERIALS
For each ornament
8x5-inch piece of white 11-count Aida cloth
Small amounts of Size 5 pearl cotton
Fiberfill, wool fabric, satin ribbon
Embroidery hoop, tapestry needle

INSTRUCTIONS

Before beginning, see the general information on pages 180–183 for special cross-stitch tips and techniques, and for materials necessary for working all counted cross-stitch projects.

The pattern, *left,* is one-fourth of border pattern. Using graph paper and markers, complete border design so that it is 55 stitches wide and 31 stitches high. Chart greeting in center.

Measure 1½ inches down from the top and 1½ inches in from left side of fabric. Begin stitching upper-left corner of border here.

Select five colors of pearl cotton for border design—one for each symbol. Use one strand of pearl cotton and work the cross-stitches over one thread of fabric. Stitch greeting in a sixth color.

See the general directions on pages 186–187 for completing an ornament.

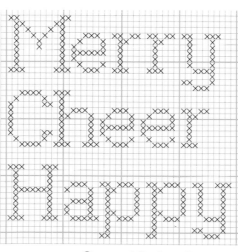

Seasonal Sayings Ornaments

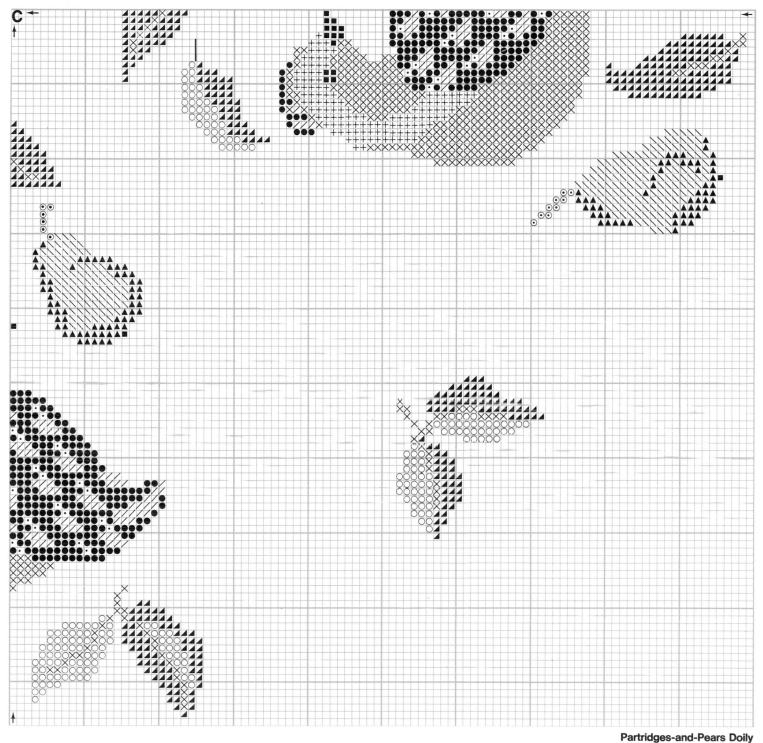

Partridges-and-Pears Doily

COLOR KEY

- ⊡ White
- ◼ Black (310)
- ◿ Rose (335)
- ⊠ Pale Brown (435)
- ◣ Kelly Green (702)
- ⊘ Bright Chartreuse (704)
- ⊞ Topaz (725)
- ▲ Light Tangerine (742)
- ◿ Medium Yellow (743)
- ◎ Dark Topaz (781)
- ⬤ Garnet (816)

Medallion Ornaments

Shown on page 141.
Finished diameter of geometric motif is 1⅞ inches; diameter of floral motif is 3 inches.
Geometric design is 33x33 stitches; floral design is 53x53 stitches.

MATERIALS
Scraps of white 18-count Aida cloth
Small amounts of embroidery floss in colors indicated below patterns
Fabric for backing, piping, and ruffles
Fiberfill, satin ribbon
Embroidery hoop
Tapestry needle

INSTRUCTIONS
Before beginning, see the general information on pages 180–183 for special cross-stitch tips and techniques, and for materials necessary for working all counted cross-stitch projects.

The patterns, *below,* are quadrants of the design. Chart entire design on graph paper. Mark horizontal and vertical centers. Baste horizontal and vertical centers of fabric.

Use two plies of floss and work the cross-stitches over one thread of the fabric.

When stitchery is completed, steam-press on wrong side.

See general directions on pages 186–187 for completing an ornament.

Geometric Medallion Ornaments

COLOR KEY
⊡	Rose	⊞	Dark Blue
⊠	Deep Rose	☑	Medium Green
⊚	Light Blue	◪	Light Yellow

Deck-the-Halls Table Mat

Shown on page 142.
Finished size of stitchery is 12x12 inches. Mat is 12¾x12¾ inches, including fringe.
Design is 176x176 stitches.

MATERIALS
19x19-inch piece of white 14-count Aida cloth
DMC embroidery floss: 1 skein *each* of black (310), deep pistachio green (319), medium pistachio green (320), medium wedgwood blue (517), light old gold (676), deep coral red (817), and medium golden brown (976)

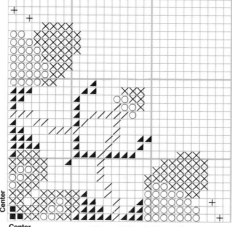

Floral Medallion Ornament

COLOR KEY
⊠	Red	☑	Light Green
⊚	Pink	⊞	Purple
◪	Medium Green	■	Gold

Tapestry needle
Embroidery hoop

INSTRUCTIONS
Before beginning, see the general information on pages 180–183 for special cross-stitch tips and techniques, and for materials necessary for working all counted cross-stitch projects.

The pattern, pages 154–155, represents one edge of table mat. Using graph paper and felt-tip markers, chart one side of mat. Then, using partial motifs on pattern as reference points, chart remaining three sides. Mark horizontal and vertical centers of chart.

Baste horizontal and vertical centers of cloth. Use two plies of floss to work the cross-stitches over one thread of cloth.

For backstitches, use a single ply of golden brown (976) to outline candle flame, a single ply of black (310) to outline candle. Use two plies of blue (517) for portions of lettering, two plies of red (817) for berries inside letters, and two plies of dark green (319) for greenery at base of candle.

Steam-press mat on wrong side.

Trim mat carefully between threads as indicated by heavy lines on pattern. Clip inside corners as indicated. To make fringe, remove threads up to dotted line.

Partridges-and-Pears Doily

Shown on page 143.
Finished diameter of stitchery is 13¾ inches. Doily is 15¾ inches in diameter, including edging.
Design is 196x196 stitches.

MATERIALS
18x18-inch piece of white 18-count Aida cloth

DMC embroidery floss: 1 skein *each* of white, black (310), rose (335), pale brown (435), kelly green (702), bright chartreuse (704), topaz (725), light tangerine (742), medium yellow (743), dark topaz (781), and garnet (816)

Jumbo rickrack
1½ yards white bias tape
White sewing thread
Embroidery hoop
Tapestry needle

INSTRUCTIONS

Before beginning, see the general information on pages 180–183 for special cross-stitch tips and techniques, and for materials necessary for working all counted cross-stitch projects.

Refer to instructions for Golden-Bells Doily, below, and graph entire doily design, using pattern, page 151.

Use three plies of floss and work the cross-stitches over one thread of Aida cloth. Mark center stitch on fabric square and stitch motifs from center point.

Steam-press the stitchery on the wrong side.

With water-erasable marking pencil, draw a 15¼-inch-diameter circle, centering motifs inside. Using jumbo rickrack, finish edges as for Golden-Bells Doily.

Golden-Bells Doily

Shown on page 143.
Finished diameter of stitchery is 9½ inches. Doily is 10⅞ inches in diameter, including edging.
Design is 135x135 stitches.

MATERIALS

12x12-inch piece of white 14-count Aida cloth
DMC embroidery floss: 1 skein *each* of black (310), Christmas red (321), dark Christmas red (498), dark

seafoam green (561), seafoam green (562), medium yellow (743), and medium cornflower blue (793)

Medium rickrack
White bias tape, white sewing thread
Embroidery hoop
Tapestry needle

INSTRUCTIONS

Before beginning, see the general information on pages 180–183 for special cross-stitch tips and techniques, and for materials necessary for working all counted cross-stitch projects.

Use three plies of floss and work the cross-stitches over one thread of Aida cloth.

Mark center stitch on fabric square and stitch motifs from center point.

The pattern, *below,* is a quadrant of the complete design. Use graph paper to chart entire doily design before stitching. To chart a design centered on a row of stitches, first chart quadrant as shown. The designated square in upper-left corner of chart is center stitch of doily design. Note that the sequence of stitches directly below this square and that of the row directly to the right are identical; these rows

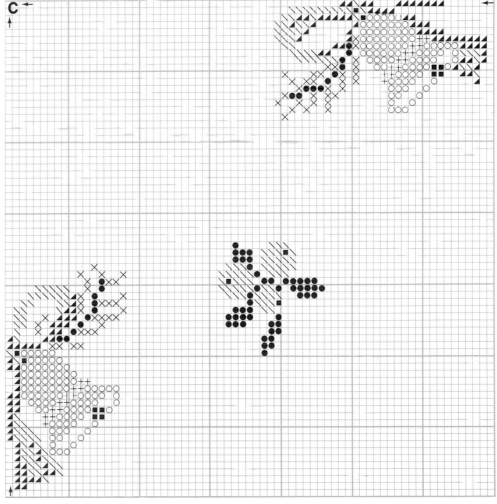

COLOR KEY

◼ Black (310)	⊠ Seafoam Green (562)
◨ Christmas Red (321)	◯ Medium Yellow (743)
◪ Dark Christmas Red (498)	⊞ Medium Cornflower Blue (793)
⬤ Dark Seafoam Green (561)	

Golden Bells Doily

form the center of the bells motif. Repeat quadrant three more times, turning pattern a quarter-turn each time, and using outermost rows of pattern as a reference point.

Wash doily, if necessary, and steam-press stitchery on wrong side.

With water-erasable marking pencil, center and draw a 10½-inch-diameter circle. Center width of rickrack along circle with right side of stitchery up (only the points show on finished rickrack edging); baste in place. Fold and overlap ends of rickrack neatly. Layer white bias tape atop rickrack; machine-stitch. Trim away excess Aida cloth. Turn bias tape to wrong

side; press. Topstitch around, securing bias tape.

Holly and Poinsettia Guest Towels

Shown on page 144.
Holly design is 88 stitches wide and 27 stitches high. Poinsettia design is 110 stitches wide and 26 stitches high.

MATERIALS
For a pair of towels
Two terry cloth hand towels with even-weave fabric bands
DMC embroidery floss: 1 skein *each* of bright Christmas red (666), light Christmas green (701), and topaz (725)
Embroidery hoop
Tapestry needle

INSTRUCTIONS
Before beginning, see the general information on pages 180–183 for special cross-stitch tips and techniques, and for materials necessary for work-

ing all counted cross-stitch projects.

Referring to the patterns, page 157, chart designs on graph paper. Mark centers. Baste centers of even-weave band on towels.

Use three plies of floss and work the cross-stitches over one thread of even-weave.

Stitch red French knots at dots on holly design and yellow French knots at dots on poinsettia design. Add checks or stripes along border.

Christmas Stocking

Shown on page 144.
Finished size is 21½ inches high.

MATERIALS
7x24-inch piece of white hardanger
DMC embroidery floss: 1 skein *each* of bright Christmas red (666), light Christmas green (701), topaz (725)
½ yard *each* of red corduroy, print fabric (lining and piping), and fleece
Cable cord

INSTRUCTIONS
Before beginning, see the general information on pages 180–183 for special cross-stitch tips and techniques, and for materials necessary for working all counted cross-stitch projects.

Referring to the pattern for Guest Towel, page 157, chart either the holly

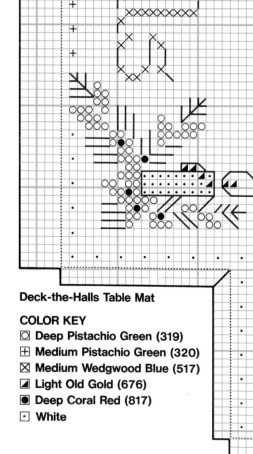

Deck-the-Halls Table Mat

COLOR KEY
◨ **Deep Pistachio Green (319)**
⊞ **Medium Pistachio Green (320)**
⊠ **Medium Wedgwood Blue (517)**
◪ **Light Old Gold (676)**
● **Deep Coral Red (817)**
⊡ **White**

leaf motif or the poinsettia motif on graph paper. Add family names, date, or other greeting to right side of flower design. Mark horizontal and vertical centers of design.

Baste centers of hardanger. Stitch design. Use three plies of floss and work the cross-stitches over two threads of fabric.

Steam-press the stocking front on the wrong side.

ASSEMBLY: Enlarge stocking pattern, page 157; add ½-inch seam allowances to shape. Use ½-inch seams.

Cut out stocking front from corduroy, print, and fleece; cut out back from corduroy and print. Stitch fleece to front, ½ inch from edge.

Make print piping. Sew piping to front along stitched line, omitting top edge. With right sides facing, sew stocking front to back along piping line. Trim seams, clip curves, turn, and press.

Sew lining together, leaving top open and a 6-inch opening at bottom. Trim seams and clip curves. Set aside.

For cuff, lay stitchery atop fleece. Baste a 21x5½-inch rectangle on stitchery, centering motif. Trim ½ inch past basting. Cut cuff lining to same size. With right sides facing, sew ends of cuff together. Repeat for cuff lining.

Sew piping to bottom basting line of cuff. With right sides facing and matching center back seams, sew lining to cuff along piping line. Trim and clip seams; turn and press. Baste raw edges together. Center and stitch cuff to stocking. Sew piping to top.

For loop, cut a 2x6-inch corduroy strip. Press to wrong side ¼ inch along long sides. Press in half lengthwise with wrong sides together and stitch closed.

Slip stocking with cuff into lining, matching side seams (right sides will be facing). Stitch. Trim and clip seams. Pull stocking through bottom opening of lining. Slip-stitch lining closed. Smooth lining into stocking. Roll up cuff and topstitch ¼ inch below piping through stocking and lining. Turn down cuff and press.

Christmas-Greetings Wall Hanging

Shown on page 145.
Finished size is 8⅛x10 inches.
Design is 75 stitches wide and 91 stitches high.

MATERIALS
16x18-inch piece of white 18-count Aida cloth
Susan Bates Anchor embroidery floss: 1 skein *each* of burgundy (44), dark green (246), gold (309), gray (401), light green (243), red (47), and yellow (307)
Embroidery hoop, tapestry needle

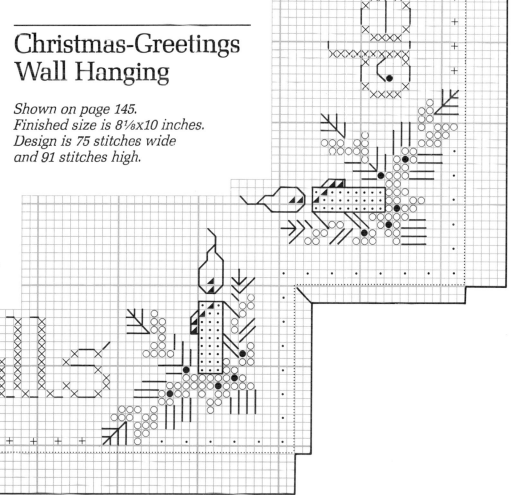

COLOR KEY
- ⊠ Burgundy (044)
- ◢ Dark Green (0246)
- ● Gold (0309)
- ■ Gray (0401)
- ⧄ Light Green (0243)
- ◯ Red (047)
- ⊡ Yellow (0307)

Christmas Greetings Wall Hanging

INSTRUCTIONS

Before beginning, see the general information on pages 180–183 for special cross-stitch tips and techniques, and for materials necessary for working all counted cross-stitch projects.

Referring to the pattern, page 156, chart design onto graph paper.

Use three plies of floss and work the cross-stitches over two threads of Aida cloth. Measure 4 inches down from the top and 4 inches in from left side; begin stitching upper-left corner of border here.

Frame the wall hanging as desired.

Greeting Card

Shown on page 145.
Finished size of stitchery is
4⅜x2¼ inches.
Design is 63x33 stitches.

MATERIALS

4x6-inch piece of perforated paper
Small amounts of embroidery floss
   in same colors as Christmas-
   Greetings Wall Hanging
   (instructions begin page 155)
Blank greeting card, spray adhesive
Tapestry needle

INSTRUCTIONS

Use three plies of floss.

Measure ¾ inch down from the top and ¾ inch in from left side of paper; begin stitching upper-left corner of border here. Work burgundy border to 63 stitches wide and 33 stitches high. Referring to pattern for Christmas-Greetings Wall Hanging, page 156, stitch greeting and candle motif from upper portion of chart, inside border.

Trim paper ⅜ inch past border. Affix stitchery to card with adhesive.

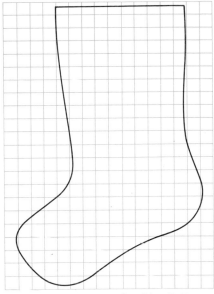

Stocking Pattern
1-Square = 1-Inch

COLOR KEYS   **Guest Towels**

◎ Bright Christmas Red (666)   ☒ Light Christmas Green (701)

A Fairyland Cottage With All the Trimmings

Resplendent with architectural gingerbread, tracery, and old-world charm, the projects in this chapter have fairy-tale beginnings. The cottage and its related designs are unusually imaginative examples of stitchery that are further embellished with a wonderful assortment of laces, beads, appliqués, and ribbons.

The cottage-shaped box *opposite* is a one-of-a-kind stitchery project that combines several techniques.

Stitch the components on even-weave fabric, and embellish them as desired. To assemble, back each stitchery with cardboard and batting and sew them together.

Instructions begin on page 162.

The pattern for the front of the cottage on the preceding pages is the basis for the sampler *opposite*. On the sampler, the addition of stitched lines that define the sides of the house, a roofline with gingerbread eaves, and a handsome chimney all combine to turn the three-dimensional shape into a two-dimensional image.

As with the cottage, the addition of laces, beads, and other trims makes the house design even more special. And a stitched-on border of lace adds a delicate framing touch.

The pattern for the oversize place mat, *above,* is taken from the sampler *opposite.* It's a simple alphabet motif that's made cheery with some heart and flower motifs.

The decorative borders at the top and bottom of the sampler are ideal patterns for edging a variety of items. For example, the repeated flower motif makes a lovely trim for a child's garment—change the color of the petals for variety.

Edge a napkin, a table runner, or curtain border in the trailing green vine with its delicate yellow blossoms. For a special brunch or luncheon, make place cards by using the alphabet to stitch each guest's name on a perforated paper card; add the flower basket motif from the front of the cottage beneath the name or a combination of other designs from the sampler.

160

COLOR KEY

White

Christmas Red (321)

Deep Coffee Brown (898)

Kelly Green (702)

Light Topaz (726)

Medium Pink (776)

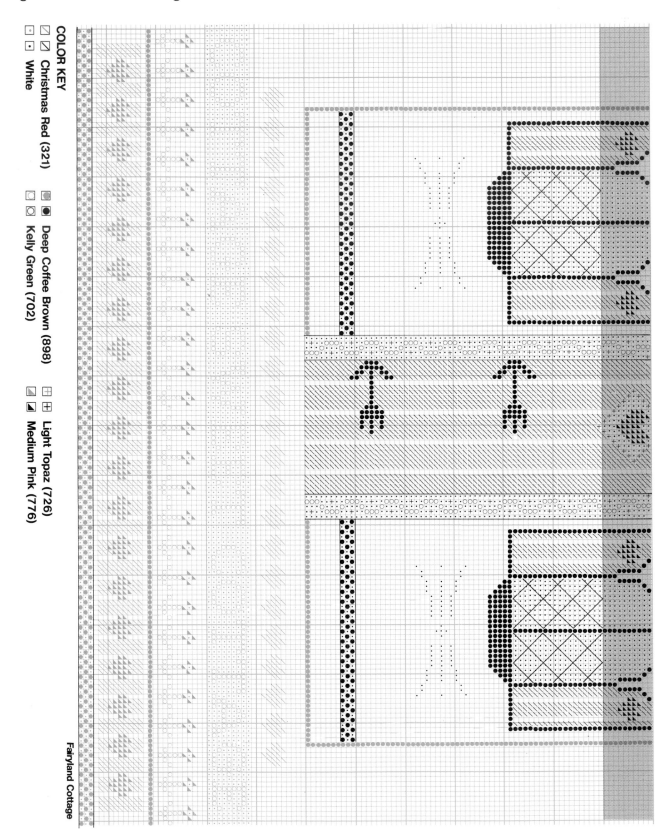

Fairyland Cottage

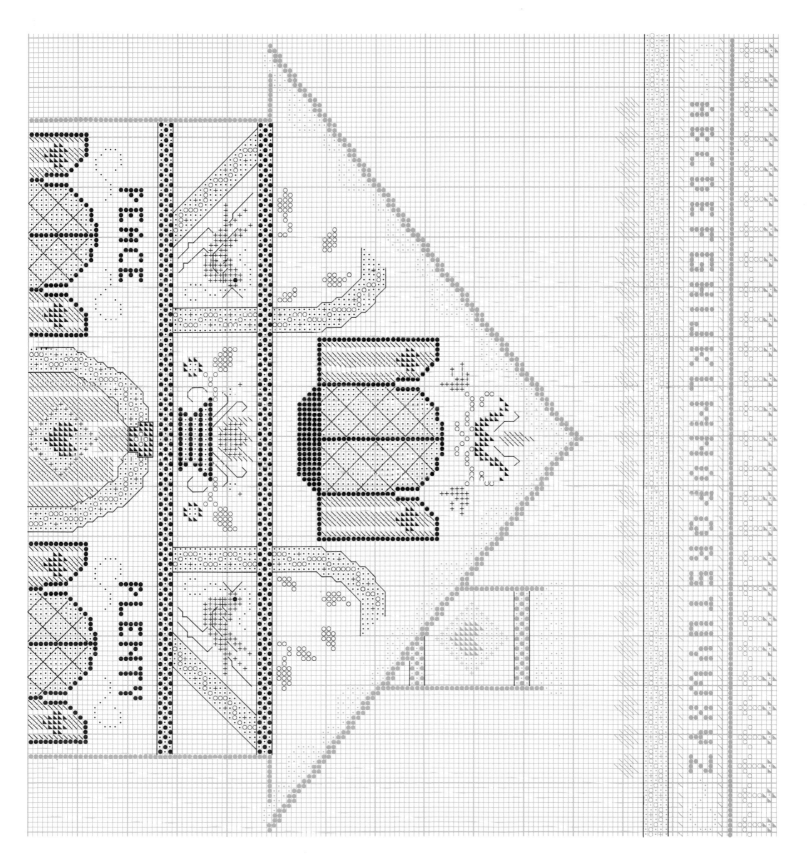

163

Cottage Box

Shown on page 159.
Finished size is approximately 9 inches wide and 10 inches long at base. Finished height is approximately 14 inches.

MATERIALS

Pieces of tan 14-count Aida cloth in the following quantities and sizes: two 12x15-inch pieces (ends), two 15x10-inch pieces (sides), two 12x16-inch pieces (roof), and four 6x7-inch pieces (chimney)

DMC embroidery floss: 3 skeins of Christmas red (321); 2 skeins *each* of white and deep coffee brown (898); and 1 skein *each* of kelly green (702), light topaz (726), and medium pink (776)

Assorted white lace in ¼-, ⅜-, and ½-inch widths

Assorted flower appliqués in white, pink, and red

Gold seed beads, small wooden bead

Key-shaped buttons, ribbon scraps

36x42-inch piece of mat board

36x42-inch piece of heavy quilt batting

1 yard muslin

Sewing thread to match Aida cloth

Crafts knife, glue

Embroidery hoop

Tapestry needle

INSTRUCTIONS

Before beginning, see the general information on pages 180–183 for special cross-stitch tips and techniques, and for materials necessary for working all counted cross-stitch projects.

Referring to patterns for cottage front, sides, roof, and chimney, chart designs onto graph paper. For front of cottage, use only the symbols printed in black; tinted symbols are for Cottage Sweet Cottage Sampler (instructions begin on page 167). Omit cat in window on one side, if desired. For roof, repeat patterns from left to right until stitchery covers a 13x8½-inch area on fabric.

Stitch design onto appropriate pieces of Aida cloth (see Materials, above). Use two plies of floss and work the cross-stitches over one thread of fabric.

Work backstitches on front of cottage as indicated on chart, using two plies of deep coffee brown (898). Work backstitches on sides of cottage as indicated, using two plies of deep coffee brown (898) along edges of beams and kelly green (702) for leaves and stems of flowers.

When stitcheries are completed, steam-press each piece on the wrong side. (*Note:* The back of the house remains unstitched.)

Lay out house front and sides on a work surface. Position flower appliqués in window boxes, in center of leaf clusters, and at end of backstitched stems; hand-tack in place. Stitch ⅜-inch-wide lace along bottom edge of front and sides beneath brown-and-white checked border; accent with gold beads. Hand-sew a row of 11 gold beads above lower windows on front and above side window. Stitch wooden bead for doorknob. Stitch key-shaped buttons beneath doorknob; add ribbon loop.

For roof, stitch rows of lace between rows of stitched motifs as indicated on pattern.

Referring to diagram, *right,* cut house ends, sides, and roof shapes from mat board with crafts knife. Cut identical shapes from batting; glue batting to each shape. Cut an 8½x9-inch bottom.

Machine-stitch two roof sections together so that rows of hearts along top edge are ¼ inch apart. Using mat board shapes, lightly trace around front, side, and roof pieces. Stitch ½-inch-wide lace in place to define peaked edge of front. Stitch ¼-inch-wide lace around edges of roof. (*Note:*

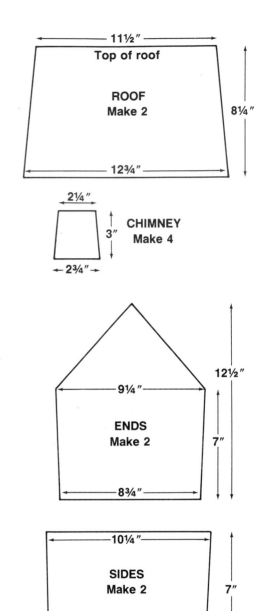

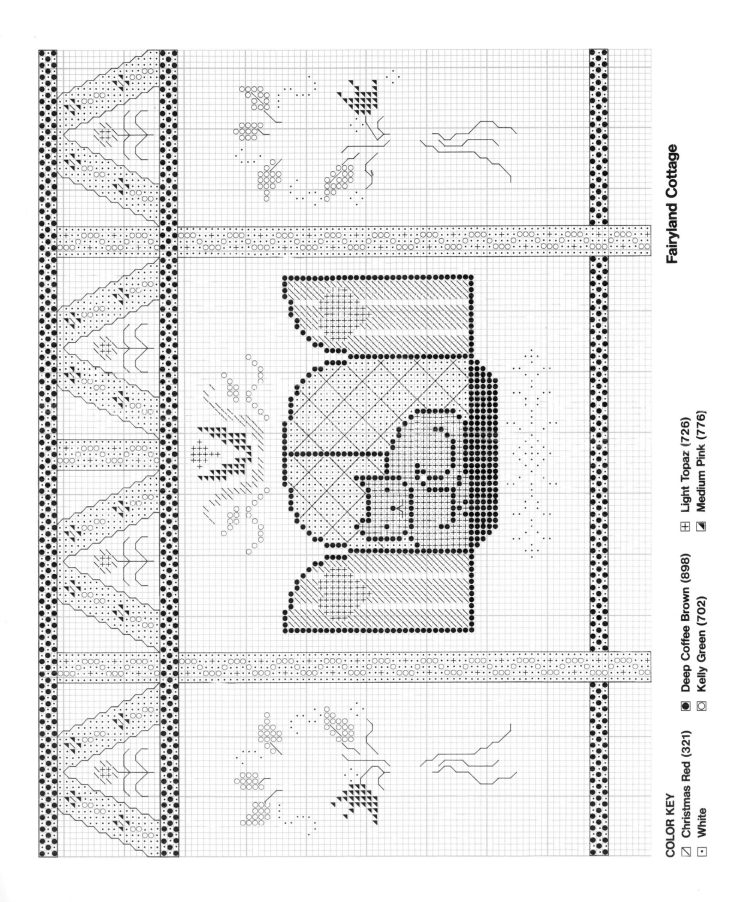

Fairyland Cottage

COLOR KEY
- ◩ Christmas Red (321)
- ⊡ White
- ◉ Deep Coffee Brown (898)
- ◎ Kelly Green (702)
- ⊞ Light Topaz (726)
- ◪ Medium Pink (776)

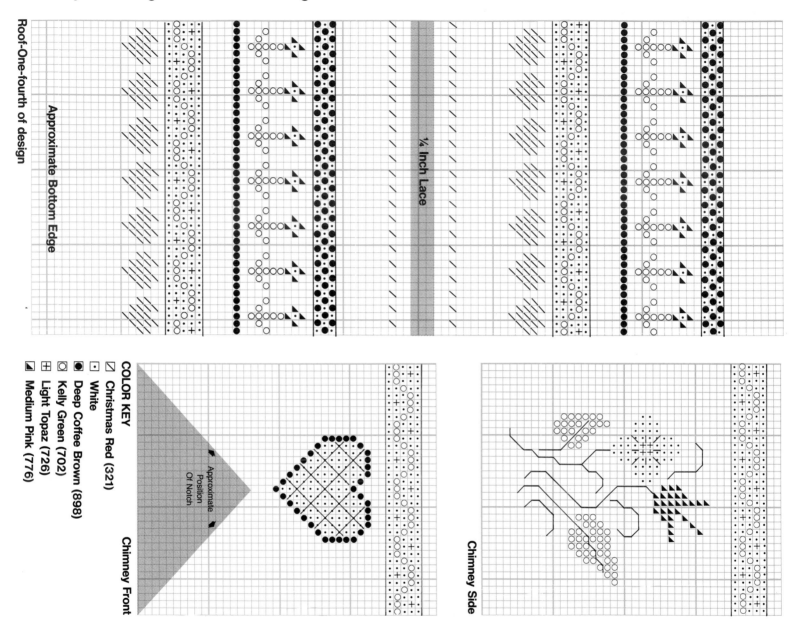

COLOR KEY

◪ Christmas Red (321)
⊡ White
● Deep Coffee Brown (898)
○ Kelly Green (702)
⊞ Light Topaz (726)
◣ Medium Pink (776)

For best results, assemble chimney after house and roof are completed.)

Cut corresponding muslin shapes ½ inch smaller. Cut muslin for roof as one piece.

Cut out shapes 1½ inches past traced lines. For each endpiece and sidepiece, center mat board shapes on wrong side of stitcheries with batting side covered. Stretch stitcheries over mat board and hold temporarily in place with masking tape. Miter points

and corners neatly. Whipstitch mitered edges together; remove masking tape. Cover bottom (which is not padded) similarly.

Turn under raw edges of muslin pieces ½ inch; press. Slip-stitch muslin to back side of ends, sides, and bottom.

Matching side seams, hand-stitch front, back, and sidepieces together. Hand-stitch bottom to ends and sides.

Cover roof pieces in the same way;

lay atop house assembly.

Cut out four chimney pieces from mat board, batting, and muslin. To determine fit of chimney, cut a piece of paper the size of one chimney section. Cut an inverted V shape to align with roof peak. Trace this V shape to two chimney sections. Glue batting to chimney sections and complete as for house shapes. Hand-stitch chimney sections together, aligning top borders. Conceal vertical seams with

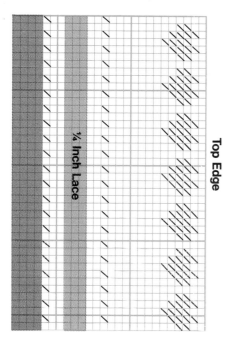

¼ Inch Lace

Top Edge

lace. Hand-stitch chimney to roof.

To assemble house so that it can be folded flat for storage, tack bottom of house in place and tack chimney to roof. Remove tacking and flatten house and chimney to store.

Cottage Sweet Cottage Sampler

Shown on page 161.
Finished size of stitchery (measured at outside edge of lace border) is 14x20½ inches.

MATERIALS
25x32-inch piece of medium brown 14-count Aida cloth
DMC embroidery floss: 2 skeins *each* of white, Christmas red (321), and deep coffee brown (898) and 1 skein *each* of kelly green (702), light topaz (726), and medium pink (776)
2 yards of ½-inch-wide white lace
White and pale yellow seed beads
Assorted flower appliqués
Yellow wooden bead for doorknob

INSTRUCTIONS
Before beginning, see the general information on pages 180–183 for special cross-stitch tips and techniques, and for materials necessary for working all counted cross-stitch projects.

Referring to the pattern, pages 162–163, chart the sampler design onto graph paper. For this sampler, include both black and tinted symbols; the color key on page 162 refers to either black or tinted symbols.

Measure 6½ inches down from top edge of fabric and 6½ inches in from left edge; begin stitching upper-left corner of sampler here. Use two plies of floss and work the cross-stitches over one thread of fabric.

Work backstitches as indicated on chart, using two plies of deep coffee brown (898).

When stitching is completed, steam-press stitchery on the wrong side.

Position flower appliqués on fabric, placing flowers in window boxes, in center of leaf clusters, and at end of backstitched stems. Stitch yellow bead to door for doorknob.

Hand-stitch white seed beads in center of each pink flower along top and bottom border of sampler, in centers of pink flowers in basket above door, and along top of chimney. Hand-stitch pale yellow seed beads over each yellow cross-stitch around door frame, along beams of upper story of house, and along lower part of upper border.

Stitch white lace past stitchery to approximately 14x20½ inches, mitering corners and adjusting slightly to make the most effective use of lace pattern repeat.

Frame the sampler as desired.

Place Mats

Shown on page 160.
Finished size is 17½x16 inches.

MATERIALS
For each place mat
22x20-inch piece of ecru 18-count Davosa fabric
DMC embroidery floss: 1 skein *each* of white, Christmas red (321), kelly green (702), light topaz (726), medium pink (776), and deep coffee brown (898)
20x18-inch piece of fleece
20x18-inch piece of muslin or print fabric (backing)
2 yards of narrow picot trim
Water-erasable marking pen
Embroidery hoop, tapestry needle

INSTRUCTIONS
Before beginning, see the general information on pages 180–183 for special cross-stitch tips and techniques, and for materials necessary for working all counted cross-stitch projects.

Referring to pattern, pages 162–163, chart top border of Cottage Sweet Cottage Sampler.

Measure 2½ inches down from top edge of fabric and 2½ inches in from left edge of fabric. Begin stitching upper-left corner of border here.

Use four plies of floss and work the cross-stitches over two threads of the fabric.

Steam-press the stitchery.

With marking pen, draw a 17½x16-inch rectangle onto right side of fabric. Position top edge of rectangle ½ inch above top of border pattern.

Line fabric with fleece and stitch layers together along marked line. Sew picot trim to stitching line. With right sides facing, sew backing fabric to stitchery, leaving an opening for turning. Trim seam allowance to ¼ inch. Clip corners; turn. Press. Slip-stitch opening closed.

Special Ways With Cross-Stitch

As with many crafts techniques, cross-stitch lends itself to innovation, experimentation, and exciting ways to embellish basic stitchery. This chapter offers several departures from traditional stitching, each with a fresh country look.

In addition to the quilt pattern border, the Home Sweet Country Home motto, *opposite,* features some surprising touches. At the base of each capital letter, small wooden beads replace stitched flowers; a bouquet of bead flowers fills in each of the bottom corners, too.

To create these flowers, fill in stems and leaves with straight stitches. Then sew on the beads at the top of each stem. An assortment of sizes and shapes makes more interesting blossoms.

Instructions for projects in this chapter begin on page 174.

The charming heart *opposite* is an example of Assisi work, a stitchery technique that calls for filling in the background around a motif instead of working the motif itself. This heart, which is ideal for a sachet or ornament, offers many options— experiment with different colored fabrics and light and dark shades of floss.

Working an allover pattern of small motifs is one way to cover a lot of area quickly, yet still create a large impact. The heart- and flower-bedecked bunnies, *above,* not only are examples of how to deftly accomplish this, but are an easy way to combine soft sculpture techniques with cross-stitching.

First stitch the motifs onto even-weave fabric. Then, outline the bunnies' bodies and ears with stem stitches; fill in the ears with satin stitches. Experienced embroiderers can create a tail by filling in a circle with turkey work; substitute a yarn pom-pom, if desired. Back the bunny with fabric, and stitch to a cardboard-backed base.

F abrics play a special role in any kind of stitchery, and cross-stitch is no exception. The color, weave, and texture of a fabric can add as much to a finished stitchery as the stitch pattern and the color and type of embroidery thread used.

The two projects shown here are examples of unconventional fabrics that make beautiful foils for cross-stitch motifs.

Choose a neutral shade of burlap for the bench cover, *right*. Most good-quality burlap is even-weave, with about 12 threads per inch. Adapt and adjust the scrolled heart motif to fit any size and shape of bench.

A humble rag rug, *opposite*, provides another out-of-the-ordinary background for some country motifs. It's stitched with cotton yarn—the warp threads of the rug form a grid to help you position the stitches evenly.

This rug, woven with white rag strips on a red cotton warp, is plain enough for complicated designs like the hearts, diamonds, and striped borders shown here. For more intricately patterned rag rugs, adapt just a portion of the pattern given, or use just one color of cotton yarn to cross-stitch the motifs.

Special Ways with Cross-Stitch

(720) (721) (722) (742) (743) (745) (701)

(963)

(893)

(817)

(3609)

(3608)

(3607) (554) (552) (550) (341) (340) (333)

COLOR KEY

- Pewter Gray (317)
- ⊠ 1 yard of each color listed
- Green (701)
- Light Christmas Green (701)
- ⊙ Dark Salmon (347)
- Extra amounts of Yellow (743)
- Light Green (704)
- -- Bright Chartreuse (704)

(701) (702) (704) (911)

(913)

(966)

(958)

(959)

(964)

(333) (794) (793) (791)

Home-Sweet-Country-Home Sampler

Home Sweet Country Home Sampler

Shown on pages 168–169.
Finished size of stitchery is approximately 13x18½ inches.
Design is 129 stitches wide and 90 stitches high.

MATERIALS

21x27-inch piece of white 18-count Aida cloth

DMC embroidery floss: 3 skeins *each* of pewter gray (317) and dark salmon (347) and 1 skein *each* of dark periwinkle blue (333), periwinkle blue (340), light periwinkle blue (341), deep violet (550), dark violet (552), light violet (554), light Christmas green (701), kelly green (702), bright chartreuse (704), dark bittersweet (720), bittersweet (721), medium bittersweet (722), light tangerine (742), medium yellow (743), light pale yellow (745), deep cornflower blue (791), medium cornflower blue (793), light cornflower blue (794), deep coral red (817), light carnation (893), medium emerald green (911), medium nile green (913), dark aqua (958), aqua (959), pale dusty rose (963), light aqua (964), medium baby green (966), dark fuchsia (3607), fuchsia (3608), and light fuchsia (3609)

Assorted small beads and buttons
Embroidery hoop, tapestry needle

INSTRUCTIONS

Before beginning, see the general information on pages 180–183 for special cross-stitch tips and techniques, and for materials necessary for working all counted cross-stitch projects.

Note: Each pinwheel requires just one yard of floss; use colors desired.

175

Referring to pattern, pages 174–175, chart design onto graph paper. Note that the symbol for each pinwheel is identical (an X); the color number for each pinwheel motif is printed in the margin. Consult materials list, *above*, for color names for each number.

Measure 4 inches down from top edge and 4 inches in from left-hand edge of fabric; begin stitching upper-left corner of border here. Stitch the pinwheels; add the greeting. Stitch, using four plies of floss and working the cross-stitches over two threads of the fabric.

Referring to pattern and photographs on pages 168–169, note position of stems and leaves. Stitch, using six plies of floss and making long running stitches. Make stems and leaves in light Christmas green (701) and bright chartreuse (704) as indicated.

Steam-press on the wrong side.

Position beads for flowers (see photographs, pages 168–169; secure in place with medium yellow (743).

Frame the sampler as desired.

Soft-Sculpture Rabbits

Shown on page 170.
Finished height is 7½ inches.

MATERIALS
For blue rabbit with pink hearts
9x11-inch piece of pale blue 14-count Aida cloth
DMC embroidery floss: 2 skeins of light turquoise (598) and 1 skein *each* of pale geranium (957) and dark aquamarine (991)

For pink rabbit with blue flowers
9x11-inch piece of pale pink 14-count Aida cloth
DMC embroidery floss: 2 skeins light salmon (761) and 1 skein *each* of pale sky blue (747) and light yellow-green (3348)

For either rabbit
¼ yard backing fabric, ¼ yard fleece
Water-erasable marking pen
Dressmaker's carbon, fiberfill
Small plastic bag filled with sand
4x6-inch piece of cardboard

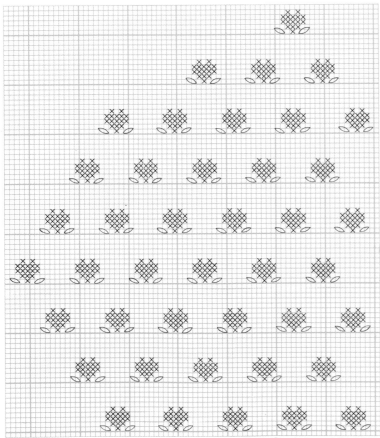

Soft-Sculptured Rabbits

COLOR KEY
⊠ Pale Geranium (957)
◟ Dark Aquamarine (991)

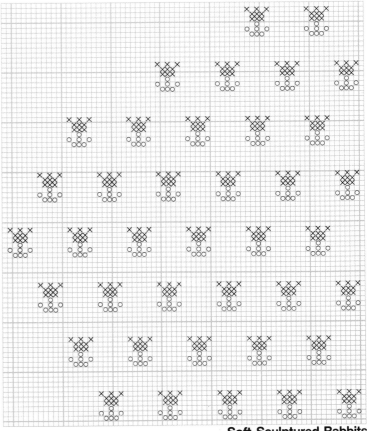

Soft-Sculptured Rabbits

COLOR KEY
⊠ Pale Sky Blue (747)
◎ Light Hunter Green (3348)

Scrap of fusible webbing
Small black bead; thread
Embroidery hoop, tapestry needle

INSTRUCTIONS

Before beginning, see the general information on pages 180–183 for special cross-stitch tips and techniques, and for materials necessary for working all counted cross-stitch projects.

Referring to patterns for rabbits, *op-posite,* work heart or flower motifs onto center of Aida cloth. Use two plies of floss and work the cross-stitches over one thread of fabric.

Trace rabbit outline, *below,* onto tissue paper. Using dressmaker's carbon, transfer outline to stitchery. Position lower-right corner of outline approximately ¼ inch beyond lower-right stitched motif. Using three plies of floss, outline rabbit with stem stitches; fill in ears with satin stitches.

Mark stitching line for rabbit approximately ¼ inch beyond embroidered outline. Pin fleece to wrong side of stitchery; machine-stitch along stitching line through all thicknesses. Pin backing to Aida cloth, right sides together. Stitch along same line, leaving bottom edge open. Clip and trim seam allowances to ¼ inch. Turn.

Sew black bead in place for eye. Stitch tail in turkey work, using six strands of floss. (*Note:* Substitute yarn or purchased pom-pom for turkey work area, if desired.) Turn under Aida cloth and backing ¼ inch along bottom edge; baste in place.

Referring to pattern for base, *below,* cut oval from cardboard and fusible webbing. Fuse a scrap of backing fabric to cardboard. Trim fabric to shape of base, adding ½-inch seam allowances. Hand-sew gathering threads in

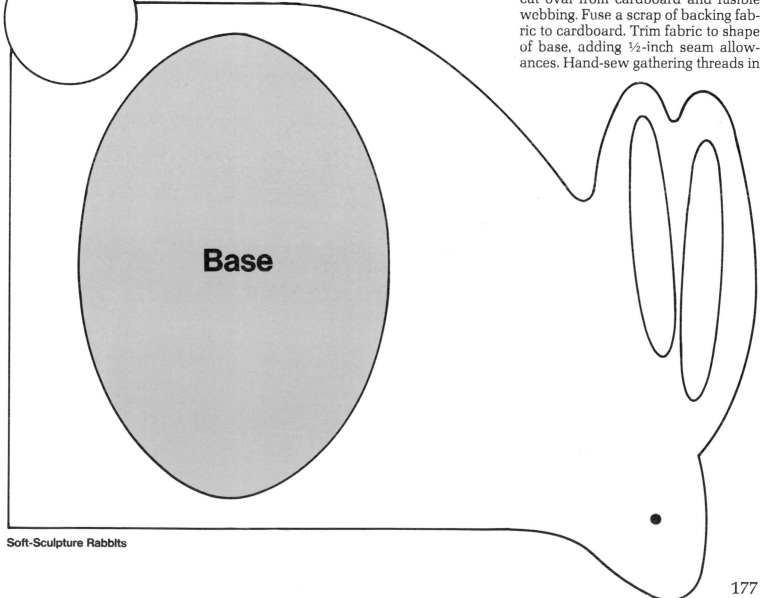

Base

Soft-Sculpture Rabbits

177

seam. Tighten gathering to shape fabric to base; knot ends.

Stuff rabbit firmly with fiberfill; add a small bag of sand at bottom for weight. Slip-stitch base to rabbit.

Heart Sachet

Shown on page 171.
Finished height is about 5 inches.
Design is 68 stitches wide and 67 stitches high.

MATERIALS
8x8-inch piece of white 14-count Aida

DMC embroidery floss: 2 skeins of any color
Bulk potpourri (*Note:* For an ornament, substitute fiberfill.)
Scrap of backing fabric
1 yard *each* of lace and piping
Scrap of satin ribbon
Embroidery hoop, tapestry needle

INSTRUCTIONS
Before beginning, see the general information on pages 180–183 for special cross-stitch tips and techniques, and for materials necessary for working all counted cross-stitch projects.

Stitch design, *below,* on hardanger. Stitch, using three plies of floss and

working the cross-stitches over one thread. (*Note:* The leaves and flowers of this pattern remain unstitched.)

Steam-press on the wrong side.

Referring to pages 186–187 for completing an ornament, assemble sachet, adding lace and piping to edges. Fill with potpourri or fiberfill. Hang from ribbon loop.

Bench Cover

Shown on page 172.
Finished size of double-heart motif is 3⅞ inches wide and 5⅛ inches high.

MATERIALS
Good-quality natural-colored burlap as large as bench top, plus 5 inches all around
Paternayan 3-ply Persian yarn (32-inch lengths): 5 strands of any color and 1 strand black (220) for each double-heart motif
Embroidery hoop
Tapestry needle

INSTRUCTIONS
Before beginning, see the general information on pages 180–183 for special cross-stitch tips and techniques, and for materials necessary for working all counted cross-stitch projects.

To begin, plan finished dimensions of bench top. Good-quality burlap has about 12 threads per inch. This design is stitched over two threads. To determine number of stitches available for bench top, multiply length and width by six. For example, the stitchery for a 15x22-inch bench will contain no more than 90x132 stitches.

Refer to the general directions for designing cross-stitch patterns on pages 184–185. Using pattern for double-heart motif, *opposite,* and number of available stitches, create pattern for bench cover. Align motifs in rows or space them equidistant for an all-

Heart Sachet

over pattern. Use colors as desired.

Stitch design, using three plies of yarn and working the cross-stitches over two threads of burlap.

Steam-press on the wrong side.

Mount stitchery on bench top and secure to base.

Rag Rug

Shown on page 173.

MATERIALS
Handwoven rag rug
Lily Sugar 'n' Cream knitting-worsted-
  weight cotton yarn
Yarn needle

INSTRUCTIONS

Before beginning, see the general information on pages 180–183 for special cross-stitch tips and techniques, and for materials necessary for working all counted cross-stitch projects.

Before stitching on rug, look closely at its weave. A handwoven rag rug will have fine cotton thread (the warp) running along its length, and rag strips (the weft) running along its width. For this project, two sizes of cross-stitches are used—the large stitches are worked over three threads of warp and over two rows of weft; the small stitches are worked over one row of warp and one row of weft.

Locate center warp thread of one end of rug and mark it with a safety pin. Count the number of warp threads from the center of the rug to each side.

Referring to pattern, *below left,* plan design. Note that the shaded squares on the pattern refer to the large stitches. Using as many motifs as will fit on rug, chart design, aligning center of rug with top point of a diamond motif or between diamond motifs.

Stitch rug, working from safety pin to each edge using one strand of yarn. Repeat the design on the other end of the rug.

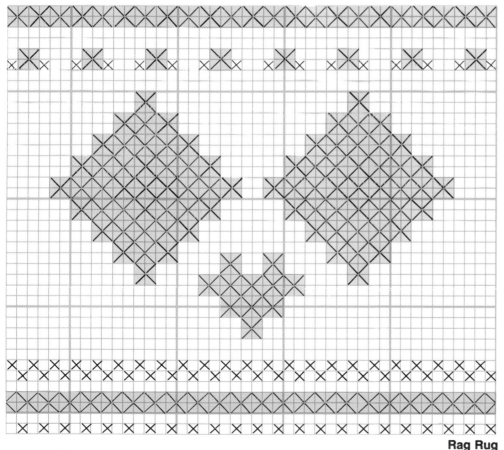

Rag Rug

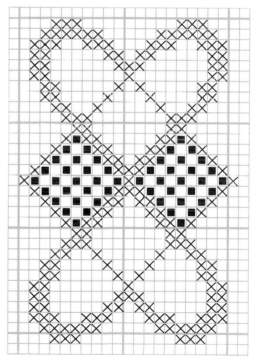

Bench Cover

COLOR KEY

⊠ Small Navy stitch: Work over 1 row of rag   ◻ Large Red stitch: Work over 2 rows of rag

⊠ Large Navy stitch: Work over 2 rows of rag   ⊠ Small Red stitch: Work over 1 row of rag

Cross-Stitch Materials

A guide to purchasing and using cross-stitch materials and equipment

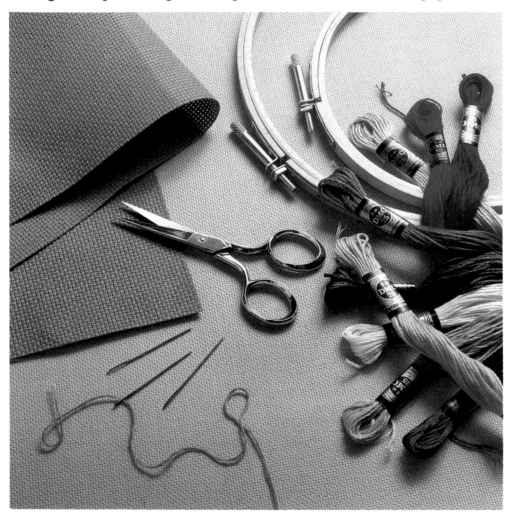

ensure uniformity of each stitch, counted cross-stitch is worked on *even-weave* fabrics.

Even-weave fabrics, which can be woven with any fibers and in various styles, feature warp and weft threads that are of a consistent thickness and uniformly spaced. This results in fabric with a consistent *thread count* at any point along its length or width.

In recent years, more and more types of even-weave fabrics have become available. Once limited to white or ecru fabrics, even-weaves today are available in a rainbow of colors, ranging from vibrant hues to beautifully subtle neutrals.

In addition to color, the choice of fiber type and texture of even-weaves has broadened. Natural fibers such as linen and cotton predominate, and these fibers, especially linen, are spun in many different ways. When choosing fabric for cross-stitch, investigate specialty fabrics that have a hand-woven look. Or, a particular design might be better suited for a flat, nondescript weave.

Instructions for most of the projects in this book specify a particular type of fabric. When making fabric substitutions, consider how changing the color, stitch count, and texture of the background will affect the overall look of the cross-stitches and finished project.

Following is a description of the major kinds of even-weave fabrics available today.

Hardanger cloth
This type of cotton even-weave fabric also is used for a type of Scandinavian embroidery; it is the namesake of a province in Norway. Because of its overall flat appearance and sturdiness, it is appropriate for working counted cross-stitch, too.

ne reason for the widespread popularity of counted cross-stitch is that the materials and equipment used to create this style of embroidery are universal. Fabric, thread, a needle, and a hoop are the only essentials. Following is a guide to selecting cross-stitch materials that will enhance your efforts and to using equipment effectively to improve your results.

Fabrics
Whatever the cross-stitch project, the fabric background of the stitchery plays a critical role. To

Unlike other types of even-weaves, hardanger varies only in color. The thread count is *always* 22 threads per inch and the weave is consistent from manufacturer to manufacturer.

Aida cloth

Aida cloth is a favorite for cross-stitchers because of the wide range of colors and thread counts. Commonly available "counts" (a reference to the number of threads per inch) of Aida cloth are 6, 8, 11, 14, and 18.

The weave of Aida cloth is distinctive because it forms easily distinguished squares across the surface of the fabric. This feature makes it an especially good choice for beginning cross-stitchers—the "holes" in the fabric (between the threads) make it easy to see where to place the cross-stitches.

Other choices

Although hardanger and Aida cloth are often the first fabrics considered for cross-stitch, other options are available.

Stores specializing in counted cross-stitch supplies carry a wide selection of linen fabrics. The beauty and durability of linen makes it ideal for stitching heirloom-quality projects. Linen fabrics have a soft luster, but are available in fewer colors; choice is limited to mostly whites, ecrus, and pastels.

Most of these fabrics, such as Lugana, are woven so that there are no distinguishable threads; they resemble ordinary fabrics. The thread counts for these fabrics are usually high, beginning at 18 threads per inch. Because of their tight, flat weaves, they are ideal for close, fine stitching.

Other popular materials for cross-stitch are perforated paper and waste canvas. Perforated paper comes in white and ecru, and has holes evenly spaced to yield 14 stitches per inch. Waste canvas, which is basted to ordinary fabrics to form a grid for stitching, resembles needlepoint canvas; it's available in many thread counts.

Flosses and threads

The array of threads available at needlework supply stores assures cross-stitchers of finding the perfect color or texture.

Embroidery floss

Six-strand embroidery floss comes in the most colors, including variegated shades.

Floss is a popular choice because it is spun so that the six plies can be separated easily. The number of plies used for a particular design depends upon the number of threads each stitch is worked over.

Pearl cotton

Pearl cotton differs from floss in that it is tightly twisted and the plies won't separate. Pearl cotton is available in three sizes—Numbers 3, 5, and 8. Number 3 is thick; Number 8 is thin. Pearl cotton has a high sheen.

Wool yarn

Most of the wool used for cross-stitch is three-ply Persian yarn. Like floss, it can be separated to adjust to the stitch count used. This type of wool is available in many colors.

Because even one ply of wool is fairly coarse, wool yarn looks best when stitched on fabrics with a relatively low thread count. Wool yarn is not as strong as cotton; cut working lengths of wool short so that it does not wear out.

Other threads

The threads mentioned above are some of the more traditional cross-stitch materials. Try working up a project with metallic threads, ribbon, fabric strips, or string.

Needles and hoops

Most needles used for cross-stitching on even-weave fabrics are *tapestry needles*. These needles feature long eyes to accommodate the bulk of embroidery threads and are blunted to simplify stitching. (A sharp pointed needle tends to split or snag fabric threads; a blunted needle more easily slides between the threads of even-weave fabrics and through the holes in perforated paper.)

Use sharp embroidery needles when working on waste canvas.

Although some purists believe counted cross-stitch should be done without a type of framed support, most cross-stitchers use a hoop. Hoops are round or oval, made of plastic, wood, or metal, and range from 3 to 23 inches in diameter.

Spring-tension hoops hold fabric tautly, as do plastic hoops, which are designed with a lip on the lower hoop to grip the fabric. Wooden or metal hoops will not hold fabric in place as tightly as plastic or spring-tension styles.

Other equipment

Other commonly available tools for cross-stitching are graph paper (10 squares per inch is a handy size to use), markers for charting designs, a ruler or a tape measure, masking tape (for binding the raw edges of even-weave fabric), and a magnifying glass designed for stitchers.

A pair of scissors, with small, sharp, pointed blades, is indispensable for embroidery.

Good Stitching

How to get professional-looking results

E ven though cross-stitch technique is relatively straightforward, all good stitchers take a few basic steps to ensure the best results: They correctly position the stitchery on the fabric, they neatly begin and end threads, and they properly form stitches whether the stitches are adjacent or separated.

Here's how to make sure your work is as attractive and durable as that of an expert.

Preparing the fabric

Preparing the fabric for stitching involves three basic steps: pressing the fabric, binding the edges, and basting.

Even-weave fabric is often sold in small pieces wrapped in plastic. Though this keeps the fabric clean, the resulting creases are sometimes difficult to remove. Pressing out the creases and folds before stitching lessens the pressing required after the fabric is stitched. (Heavy pressing over stitched areas can flatten stitches and alter the color and appearance of the design.) To remove creases, mist the fabric lightly and press with a warm iron. For stubborn folds, saturate the fabric or cover it with a wet press cloth before ironing. Or, try·applying a weak solution of vinegar and water to creases.

All fabrics unravel along cut edges while being stitched—some weaves unravel more easily than others. Raveled threads not only diminish the size of the background fabric, but are bothersome when they become tangled with the embroidery threads. Binding the edges of the fabric will eliminate raveling. The best way to bind fabric edges is with masking tape—simply fold the tape over the raw edges. An alternative to using masking tape is to machine-zigzag-stitch along the raw edges.

Regardless of the size or complexity of the stitchery, it's a good idea to add basted lines to the background to position the stitchery correctly. Depending on the nature of the chart, basted lines can be added in various ways. For a single motif, merely basting the horizontal and vertical centers is sufficient. These lines are essential for stitching a chart divided into quadrants. For complicated designs, you may wish to baste horizontal and vertical lines every 10 stitches to correspond to the bolder lines of a chart.

Flosses and yarns require less preparation than fabric, but for large or complicated projects, a little advance work can eliminate later confusion.

Floss caddies are available at needlework supply outlets. These enable a stitcher to store cut lengths of thread. They keep individual colors of floss separated, which can be important when you work with closely shaded colors of thread.

When working with many colors, it's handy to make a small card of threads before beginning. Jot the color names and numbers on an index card; tape a snippet of thread next to its corresponding label to use as a reference while stitching.

Working cross-stitches

To make a cross-stitch, pull a threaded needle from the wrong side of the fabric in a lower corner of the stitch. Carry the needle to the opposite upper corner of the stitch and insert it through the fabric from front to back. This makes the first half of the cross-stitch. (*Note:* The number of threads of fabric a stitch is worked over will vary from project to project. Consult each project's instructions for directions.)

To complete the stitch, make another stitch from opposite corners to cover the first half.

The first half of the cross-stitch may be worked from lower left to upper right *or* from lower right to upper left. In either case, make sure that all of the stitches are crossed *in the same direction*. This becomes especially important when working a quadrant pattern and the work is being turned at right angles.

Beginning and ending threads

The best way to begin a cross-stitch is by using a waste knot. It is a temporary knot and will be clipped when no longer necessary.

To begin, knot the end of your thread. Insert the needle into the *right* side of the fabric, about 4 inches from the placement of the first cross-stitch. Bring the needle up through the fabric and work the first series of cross-stitches. Stitch until the thread is used up or until the area using this color is complete.

To end a working thread, slip the needle under the previously stitched threads on the wrong side of the fabric for 1 to 1½ inches. Clip the thread.

Turn the piece to the right side and clip the beginning knot. Rethread the needle with the excess floss, push the needle through to the wrong side of the stitchery, and finish off the thread as directed above.

If you are working with areas that use a variety of thread colors (for example, a multicolored bouquet of tiny flowers), you may not wish to begin and end the thread for each flower or leaf. In these instances, carry the thread across the back of the fabric. To secure the thread, slip the threaded needle under previously stitched crosses.

When carrying threads across the back of the fabric, tension is important. If your tension is too tight, the fabric tends to bunch up; if the tension is too loose, the back becomes messy and threads may tangle and twist or leave a shadow on the front of the work.

Using charts

Most stitchers are accustomed to stitching from charts. The charts in this book feature symbols, each one representing a cross-stitch worked in a particular color. The symbols are coded in a "color key" adjacent to the chart. Each symbol on the grid represents one cross-stitch, unless specified otherwise in the instructions.

Because many of the patterns in this book are too large to fit on one page, charts may have to be "pieced" together to form the complete pattern. A shaded area on a pattern extending past a single page simply means that it is already represented on the other portion; overlap the stitches in the shaded area to complete the pattern.

Instructions in this book often state that each pattern be graphed out with colored markers before stitching. Experienced stitchers may choose to stitch directly from the pattern on the page.

Correcting mistakes

Regardless of the complexity of a design, or of a stitcher's skill, mistakes are inevitable. What to do about mistakes depends largely upon their magnitude, when they're discovered, and what is necessary to correct them.

Small errors, such as working one or two additional stitches within a shaded area or stitching the end of a leaf so that it points in an opposite direction, will usually go unnoticed.

Some areas of stitching, however, must be perfect, or the remainder of the design won't look right. When you've stitched around the border of a sampler, for example, and the corners don't align, there's little choice but to find the error and re-work the stitches.

To remove stitches, use a pair of *sharp* scissors with tiny blades. Working from the back side, carefully snip away the threads and discard them. Use a pair of tweezers to pluck away stubborn threads.

Cross-Stitch Designs

How to create your own cross-stitch patterns

You'll find that many of the cross-stitch patterns in this book can be worked up in a variety of ways. Changing the fabric or other materials, or positioning the design differently on a background provides additional options for a

stitchery. On these two pages are some hints for finding, sizing, and charting your cross-stitch patterns, along with sources for basic materials.

Sources of patterns

One popular method of designing cross-stitch—samplers, in

particular—is to combine traditional motifs in a new composition. It's relatively easy to create a border design (perhaps combining two or more border designs to make a new pattern), fill it with some beautiful alphabets and numerals toward the top of the sampler, and add a collection of motifs in the lower areas. Consult the adaptations of antique cross-stitch samplers shown on pages 98–103 for good examples of the general style for traditional samplers.

A fascinating method of incorporating authentic cross-stitch alphabets and motifs is to study examples of old needlework in your own area. Local museums and historical societies are likely to have cross-stitch samplers in their collections; ask for permission to sketch a portion of these treasured stitcheries for further reference. Referring to an illustrated catalog of the museum's collection (possibly available at a public library) is an alternative to sketching from the actual stitchery.

Establishing a stitch count

As with other types of embroidery, determining the finished size of a cross-stitch pattern is the first step to designing what will work. You may have chanced upon a beautiful frame at an antiques shop or auction that's ideal for a sampler, for example. Or you'd like to select just a portion of a large design to make a small Christmas ornament. In either case, deciding upon and working around a stitch count is necessary to create a design that will be the right size after it's stitched.

The stitch count differs from the thread count of even-weave fabric: the stitch count refers to the number of *stitches* per inch with a given combination of fabric and thread;

184

the thread count refers only to the number of threads per inch of the weave of the fabric.

For example, hardanger fabric always is woven with 22 threads per inch. Hardanger has many possible stitch counts, however. Working each cross-stitch over one thread of the fabric yields 22 stitches per inch; working a stitch over two threads yields 11 stitches per inch; working a stitch over three threads yields just under 7½ stitches per inch.

Although this sounds uncomplicated, consider the assortment of fabrics available to stitchers today. Each type of fabric has a different stitch count, and some are suitable only for stitches worked over a limited number of threads.

Selecting the correct color, weave, and texture of even-weave fabric is another challenge.

Although there are no firm rules about selecting a fabric, it's a good idea to make sure that the fabric complements the design. A simple motif can be enhanced by using a textured fabric; a complicated design might be overwhelmed by a distracting background.

Charting

Experienced stitchers claim that developing certain designs on paper before beginning to stitch can prevent mistakes later on. It's easier to first complete the second half of a mirror-image pattern on paper, for example, than rip out stitches that aren't positioned correctly.

Many designs are simple enough to work directly from a chart as it appears on a printed page. But if you graph them out on paper beforehand, you won't have to keep a bulky book or magazine handy when stitching. You'll also become more familiar with the pattern.

Quadrants

Some patterns are so large and repetitive that only portions of them are charted. Prime examples of partial patterns are those printed in fourths, or *quadrants*. These designs are based on horizontal and vertical lines. Imagine a map divided into fourths along north-south and east-west lines; the northeast, southeast, southwest, and northwest fourths of the map are its quadrants. Each fourth of a design stitched in quadrants is identical.

Working from a quadrant involves centering the design correctly on the fabric and rotating the chart one-quarter turn as each fourth of the design is stitched. For complicated designs presented in quadrants, it's a good idea to chart the entire design, or at least key elements, before beginning to stitch.

Centering Motifs

Charting a name, a date, a row of motifs, or lines of verse so that they're centered left and right involves three steps.

Note whether the main design is centered on a stitch (the width of the design is an uneven number of stitches) or between two stitches (the width of the design is an even number of stitches). Draw a center line down the middle of the master pattern.

Graph out each unit to be centered on a separate piece of graph paper. Count the number of stitches from left to right and divide by two to find the center. Draw a line along the center, either down the middle of a stitch or between stitches.

Transfer each set of words or motifs to the master pattern. Either re-chart each set or carefully tape the smaller graphs in place on the master pattern.

Sources

American sources for materials used in this book are listed below. For European sources, see page 189.

Floss
DMC Corporation
107 Trumbull St.
Elizabeth, NJ 07206

Anchor Handicrafts
212 Middlesex Ave.
Chester, CT 06412

Three-ply Persian yarn
Paternayan Yarns
Johnson Creative Arts
445 Main St.
West Townsend, MA 01474

Ribbon for cross-stitch
C.M. Offray and Son, Inc.
Rt. 24, Box 601
Chester, NJ 07930-0601

Even-weave fabrics
Charles Craft
P. O. Box 1049
Laurinburg, NC 28352

Norden Crafts
P. O. Box 1
Glenview, IL 60025

Zweigart Fabric
35 Fairfield Place
West Caldwell, NJ 07006

Perforated paper
Astor Place, Ltd.
239 Main Ave.
Stirling, NJ 07980

Accessories designed for needlework inserts
Sudberry House
P.O. Box 895
Old Lyme, CT 06371

Finishing and Displaying

How to assemble and display your work

Careful finishing will only add to the beauty of a cross-stitch design. Cleaning, pressing, and assembling a stitchery are simple steps that will also protect and preserve your work for many years to come.

Cleaning

Even the most fastidious stitchers will need to clean a completed cross-stitch piece. A stitchery may appear clean, but oils from your hands accumulate on fabric and thread and will eventually soil them.

Cross-stitched pieces may be dry-cleaned or washed by hand. One advantage to hand-laundering is that it will remove hoop marks more efficiently than dry-cleaning.

To launder a stitchery, thoroughly dissolve some detergent in cold water. Add the stitchery and gently squeeze the suds through the fabric. Rinse well in cold water (change the water rather than holding the fabric under a faucet); continue until no soap remains.

Remove excess water by rolling the piece in a towel. Don't wring the fabric; wrinkles will be difficult to remove.

Place the fabric facedown on a smooth towel (terry cloth towels may leave marks). Iron the fabric until it's dry. Ironing will give the fabric more body than allowing it to air-dry. Never dry cross-stitched fabric in a dryer.

Finishing edges

Many stitcheries intended to be used flat, such as table covers or doilies, simply require hemming so that the edges don't ravel.

For a double-fold hem, turn under the raw edge to the wrong side approximately ⅛ inch; then turn under once more ¼ inch. Finger-press the edges; baste. Hand-stitch with tiny stitches or machine-topstitch with matching thread.

To trim an edge with rickrack, mark the fabric to the desired finished dimensions on the right side of the fabric. Center the rickrack on this line, and machine-topstitch along the center edge of the rickrack. Trim the raw edges of the fabric even with the outer points of the rickrack. Turn and press rickrack to the wrong side, allowing half of the rickrack to show past the edge. Topstitch the rickrack in place.

Pillows, sachets, and ornaments

Despite the difference in size, pillows, sachets, and ornaments are assembled in the same manner.

To assemble a pillow or ornament without adding trims to the edges, simply mark the finished size on the wrong side of the stitchery. Pin a piece of backing fabric to the stitchery, right sides facing. Stitch along the outline, leaving an opening for turning. Trim the seams, turn the work, and press. Stuff with fiberfill to desired firmness. Slip-stitch the opening closed.

Making Ruffles and Piping

Ruffles and piping add a tailored touch to a three-dimensional shape. You can purchase ready-made piping and ruffling at fabric stores, but to perfectly match other fabrics and colors, you can make your own.

With striped or plaid fabric, cut the ruffle or piping strips on the straight grain, or on the bias. The choice depends on the nature of the print. Cut plain fabric on the bias— ruffles will be more graceful and piping will be easier to shape. Crosswise-cut straight-grain strips are somewhat easier to handle than those cut lengthwise.

To make ruffles, cut fabric into strips that are twice the width of the finished size *plus* twice the width of the seam allowance. (Use ½-inch seams for large items like pillows and ¼-inch seams for smaller items.) The length of the strip should be at least twice the finished length of the edge it will be stitched to. Cut strips, seam ends to form a circle, then fold in half lengthwise, keeping raw edges even; press. Machine-stitch two rows (with longest stitch setting) through both thicknesses; stitch one row directly on the seam line and the second row evenly between first row and raw edge. Pull bobbin threads to gather.

For piping, wrap a strip of fabric around cording; baste raw edges together. (Do not baste snugly against cording at this point.) Trim seam allowance to match that of ruffle.

Applying Piping and Ruffles

It's easiest to apply piping and ruffles to the right side of the stitchery before further assembly. Cut away excess fabric to form the same seam allowance as for piping/ruffle. Pin the piping/ruffle to the right side of the work, keeping the raw edges even with the edge of the stitchery. The folded edge of the ruffle and the corded edge of the piping will face the center of the stitchery, with the raw edges of both facing outward. Be sure that the ruffle fullness is evenly distributed, with extra fullness at the corners to prevent the ruffle from cupping. Baste the piping/ruffle directly over the seam line. Complete as for the untrimmed pillow above.

Framing

Heirloom stitcheries and large samplers are best displayed in frames. Covering a stitchery with glass is a matter of personal preference, but the glass should be held away from the fabric with spacers. (Moisture can be trapped inside a frame and will condensate on the inside of the glass; when fabric is wedged against glass in this way, it can rot.)

Ready-made frames are widely available in a range of sizes and styles. When selecting a ready-made frame, choose one that is in keeping with the nature of your stitchery—a simple wood frame might work best with a country-style sampler while a painted metal frame would better enhance a more contemporary stitchery.

Having a stitchery professionally framed is another option. There will be more frames to select from, and a framer can add matting.

Once you've selected a frame, though, it's easy to mount a stitchery and secure it inside the frame.

To mount a stitchery, cut a piece of ⅛- to ¼-inch-thick mounting board to the desired size. Pad the front of the board with quilt batting, if desired. Wrap the stitchery around the board. Insert pins temporarily into the edges of the board, starting at the center point of each side; add more pins, working toward the corners. Check that the lengthwise and crosswise grains of the fabric run parallel to the board.

With the piece facedown, fold the excess fabric to the wrong side; trim the excess, leaving approximately 1½ inches. Miter the corners, cutting away the excess fabric. Use a glue stick intended for fabrics to affix the fabric to the board. When the glue is dry, remove the pins.

Secure the board in the frame. Finish by gluing the paper to the back edges of the frame.

Alternatives to framing

There are other ways to display a stitchery that don't require the expense or effort of framing.

Many craft supply stores offer small wooden or plastic frames that come with a special backing piece. Just smooth the stitchery over the backing and press it in the frame.

Consider mounting a stitchery inside a wooden embroidery hoop. Putting the tension screw at the top of the design, place the stitchery in the hoop. Trim the edges and secure them in place by running a layer of glue between the inner and outer hoops. Conceal the screw with a ribbon bow and hang.

Acknowledgments

We would like to express our gratitude and appreciation to the many people who helped us with this book. Our heartfelt thanks go to each of the artists and cross-stitchers who enthusiastically contributed designs, ideas, and projects.

Thanks, also, to the photographers, whose creative talents and technical skills added much to the book. In addition, we acknowledge our debt to the companies, institutions, and individuals who provided materials for projects, locations for photography, or in some other way contributed to this book.

American readers will find a list of sources for cross-stitch supplies on page 185. European readers will find sources on page 189. If you cannot locate the threads, fabrics, or other materials you need for your projects, contact one of the sources listed for assistance.

DESIGNERS

Gary Boling—tea cozy and napkin caddy, 19; tablecloth, 20; afghan, 21; cherry napkin, 56; cherry picture frames, 57; initial pin, 64; hand mirror, 64; candle screen, 64; bolster and curtain tiebacks, 66–67; guest towels, 120; sampler, 121; bed skirt and blanket edging, 122; shelf liners, 123; ornaments, 140; floral medallion ornament; 141.

Laura Collins—animal figures, 86–87.

Dixie Falls—tablecloth, sachet, and towels, 62-63; name plaques, 89; wall hanging and card, 145

Diane Hayes—sampler, 110-111; tablecloth, 136-137.

Jane Kennelly and Lorraine Smith (Jane & Lori Designs)—table mat, 142.

Alla Ladyzhensky—doilies, 143.

Linda Lindgren—towel borders, 144.

Maureen LoPresti—wedding sampler, 37.

Margaret Sindelar—apron, 17; luggage tag, 81; map case, 81; soft-sculpture rabbits, 170.

Patricia Sparks—mitten holder, 88; cottage, 158–159.

Ciba Vaughan—geometric medallion ornament, 141.

Jim Williams—Prairie Blooms sampler and motifs, 14–23; cherry shelf liner and sampler, 54–55; flower-and-leaf motif, 64–65; rectangular pillows, 66–67; cherry place mat, 56; Woodland Blossoms motifs, 118–125;

ornaments and stocking, 138–139; heart, 171.

Dee Wittmack—trivet, 42; housewarming sampler, 43; monogramming alphabet, 64–65; throw, 68–69; sampler and accessories, 78–81; alphabet, 90–91; picnic basket and album cover, 112–113; sampler, 161; sampler, 168–169; bench cover, 172; rug, 173.

Mary Zdrodowski—birth announcement wall hanging and pillow, 40–41.

PHOTOGRAPHERS

Hopkins Associates—14–23, 36–43, 54–57, 99, 118–125, 136–140, 144, 180–187.
Sean Fitzgerald—64–67

Michael Jensen—62–63, 98–101, 141–145, 158–161.
Perry Struse—Cover, 6–13, 36, 54, 68–69, 78–81, 86–91, 102–103, 110–113, 120, 158, 168–173.

ACKNOWLEDGMENTS

Laura Ashley (tea set, pages 68–69)
714 Madison Avenue
New York, NY 10021

Dwight and Joan Axtell

Mary Lamb Becker

Patricia Bradshaw

Jerry Brown
The Christopher Inn,
Excelsior, Minnesota

Laura Collins

Heather Cravens

Christopher Cravens

Roger and Carol Dahlstrom

Des Moines Water Works,
   Des Moines, Iowa

Des Moines Department of Parks
and Recreation

Dot's Frame Shop
Des Moines, Iowa

Germaine Eagleton

Phillip and Kathy Engel

Linda Emmerson

Donna Clas

Sandy Guely

Jim and Barbara Forbes

Janelle Hansen

Eleanor Hart

Dorothy Hohnbaum

Arne Jorgenson

Katherine Kauzlarich

Richard Latch

Corinne Oleson
paper white, ltd. (lace tablecloth
   and picture frame,

pages 62 and 63)
P.O. Box 956
Fairfax, CA 94930
Patricia Ptasnik

Schumaker's New Prague Inn
New Prague, Minnesota

Sam and Becky Senti

Margaret Sindelar

Rosa Snyder

Diane Upah

Pam Wagner

Wamsutta (bed linens,
   pages 118–121)
111 West 40th St.
New York, NY 10018

SOURCES ABROAD

Floss
   Dollfus-Mieg et Cie "D.M.C."
   DMC Corporation
   88, Rue de Rivoli - 75004
   Paris, France

   J. & P. Coats Ltd.
   C.D.M.D.
   39 Durham St.
   Kinning Park
   Glasgow, Scotland G41-1BS

Ribbon for cross-stitch
   C. M. Offray and Son, Ltd
   Fir Tree Place
   Church Road
   Ashford, Middlesex
   England TW15-2PH
Perforated paper
   The Silver Thimble

The Old Malt House
Clarence Street
Bath, Avon
England BA15NS
Even-weave fabrics
   Zweigart in Germany
   P. O. Box 120
   7032 Sindelfingen
   West Germany

INDEX

Page numbers in **bold** type refer to pictures with accompanying text. The remaining numbers refer to how-to instructions.

INDEX

Have BETTER HOMES
AND GARDENS® magazine
delivered to your door.
For information, write to:
MR. ROBERT AUSTIN
P.O. BOX 4536
DES MOINES, IA 50336